Copyright © 2023 by Jonathan A. Sinclair (Author)

This book is protected by copyright law and is intended solely for personal use. Reproduction, distribution, or any other form of use requires the written permission of the author. The information presented in this book is for educational and entertainment purposes only, and while every effort has been made to ensure its accuracy and completeness, no guarantees are made. The author is not providing legal, financial, medical, or professional advice, and readers should consult with a licensed professional before implementing any of the techniques discussed in this book. The content in this book has been sourced from various reliable sources, but readers should exercise their own judgment when using this information. The author is not responsible for any losses, direct or indirect, that may occur from the use of this book, including but not limited to errors, omissions, or inaccuracies.

We hope this book has been informative and helpful on your journey to understanding and celebrating older adults. Thank you for your interest and support!

Title: Fallen Stars: The Untold Stories of Troubled Number 1 Draft Picks (1960-1980)
Subtitle: The Rise, Struggles, and Quiet Exits of NBA's Most Disappointing Rookies

Series: Lost Potential: The Troubled Legacy of Number 1 Draft Picks in the NBA (1960-1980)
By Jonathan A. Sinclair

Table of Contents

Introduction 6
Overview of the book's purpose and focus 6
Significance of number 1 draft picks and their expectations 9
Historical context of the NBA during 1960-1980 13

Chapter 1: LaRue Martin, picked in 1972, retired in 1976 17
Early life and rise to basketball prominence 17
The anticipation surrounding his selection as the number 1 pick 20
Initial struggles and challenges faced in the NBA 23
Failed attempts at redemption and eventual retirement 27

Chapter 2: Joe Barry Carroll, picked in 1980, retired in 1991 31
Background and college success leading to high expectations 31
The pressure of living up to the number 1 pick status 35
Promising moments and underwhelming performances 39
The impact of off-court factors on his career trajectory. 43

Chapter 3: Austin Carr, picked in 1971, retired in 1981 47

    Collegiate stardom and high hopes as a number 1 draft pick *47*

    Initial success and glimpses of potential in the NBA *51*

    Injuries and setbacks derailing his progress *54*

    Coping with unfulfilled expectations and life after retirement *57*

Chapter 4: Fred Hetzel, picked in 1965, retired in 1971 .... **61**

    The story of Fred Hetzel's journey from college to the NBA *61*

    Struggles with injuries and inconsistency in the league. 66

    The impact of external factors on his performance *70*

    Reflections on a career that fell short of expectations *74*

Chapter 5: Tom Burleson, picked in 1974, retired in 1981 .... **77**

    Tom Burleson's background and college achievements . *77*

    Challenges faced in transitioning to the professional level *80*

    Injury struggles and their impact on his career *83*

    The decision to retire and the legacy he left behind *86*

Chapter 6: Exploring the common themes and lessons **89**

    Analyzing the shared experiences of these number 1 draft picks *89*

The pressure of expectations and its effects on player development *92*
Reflections on the challenges and setbacks faced by these players *96*
Identifying patterns and factors contributing to their underwhelming careers *99*

Chapter 7: Impact and Aftermath **102**
Examining the long-term consequences for the players and the league *102*
How the legacies of these number 1 picks have been remembered *106*
Lessons learned and changes implemented in the NBA draft system *109*
The enduring impact on future generations of players .113

Conclusion **117**
Recap of the book's key points and findings *117*
Final thoughts on the troubled legacies of number 1 draft picks *120*
Reflecting on the broader significance and implications of their stories *123*

Key Terms and Definitions **127**
Supporting Materials **129**

Introduction

Overview of the book's purpose and focus

The NBA Draft is a highly anticipated event that holds the promise of transforming the fortunes of struggling franchises. Every year, the number 1 draft pick is hailed as the future of a team, the chosen one who will lead them to glory. However, history has shown that being selected as the top pick does not guarantee success. In fact, there is a long list of players who failed to live up to the immense expectations placed upon them.

In "Fallen Stars: The Untold Stories of Troubled Number 1 Draft Picks (1960-1980)," we embark on a journey through the captivating narratives of the fallen stars of the NBA. This book seeks to uncover the forgotten stories and troubled legacies that shaped an era, focusing on the number 1 draft picks from 1960 to 1980. During this period, the NBA was undergoing significant changes, both on and off the court, and the pressures faced by these highly anticipated rookies were immense.

The purpose of this book is twofold. Firstly, it aims to shed light on the lives and careers of these number 1 draft picks who failed to meet the lofty expectations placed upon them. By delving into their personal stories, we explore the dreams shattered and the struggles faced by these individuals, revealing the emotional toll of immense pressure and the weight of unfulfilled potential.

Secondly, "Fallen Stars" offers a poignant reflection on the true measure of greatness in professional basketball. It questions the widely held notion that success in the NBA can be solely determined by draft position and statistical achievements. Through the exploration of these troubled legacies, we challenge the notion that greatness is solely defined by on-court accolades, urging readers to consider the broader context in which these players lived and the impact of external factors on their careers.

Throughout the book, we will examine the stories of LaRue Martin, Joe Barry Carroll, Austin Carr, Fred Hetzel, Tom Burleson, and others who rose to prominence as number 1 draft picks but ultimately fell short of expectations. These players represent a diverse range of backgrounds, experiences, and challenges, providing valuable insights into the complex and unpredictable nature of professional sports.

By analyzing the shared experiences of these fallen stars, we aim to uncover common themes and lessons. The pressure of expectations, the challenges faced in transitioning to the professional level, and the impact of off-court factors on player development are just a few of the subjects explored. Through these narratives, we hope to offer a deeper understanding of the fragile nature of success and the enduring impact it has on the lives of these athletes.

"Fallen Stars" also seeks to examine the long-term consequences for the players and the league. We will reflect on how these number 1 draft picks have been remembered and the lessons learned from their troubled legacies. Additionally, we will explore any changes implemented in the NBA draft system as a result of these experiences and the enduring impact they have had on future generations of players.

In conclusion, "Fallen Stars: The Untold Stories of Troubled Number 1 Draft Picks (1960-1980)" uncovers the captivating stories and troubled legacies that shaped an era in the NBA. Through a comprehensive exploration of the lives and careers of these fallen stars, we challenge conventional notions of success and greatness in professional basketball. By delving into their struggles, we hope to provoke thoughtful reflection on the true measure of greatness and the complexities faced by those who dare to dream on the court. Join us on this enthralling journey as we uncover the forgotten stories that lie beneath the surface of the NBA's history.

Significance of number 1 draft picks and their expectations

In the world of professional basketball, the number 1 draft pick holds a special significance. The player selected with this prestigious honor is often seen as a savior, a franchise-altering talent who has the potential to transform the fortunes of a struggling team. However, the weight of expectations placed upon these individuals can be immense, leading to both great triumphs and devastating disappointments.

In "Fallen Stars: The Untold Stories of Troubled Number 1 Draft Picks (1960-1980)," we delve into the captivating narratives of the fallen stars of the NBA. Before we embark on their individual journeys, it is crucial to understand the significance of number 1 draft picks and the extraordinary expectations that come with this distinction.

The number 1 draft pick is not simply a title; it represents a gateway to hope and aspirations for a team and its fan base. Franchises invest a great deal of time, resources, and scouting efforts in identifying the player they believe possesses the talent, potential, and character to become the cornerstone of their future success. The number 1 draft pick is often viewed as a rare opportunity to secure a generational talent, someone who can instantly elevate a team's performance and bring them closer to championship glory.

The expectations placed upon number 1 draft picks are not solely the product of team aspirations, but also the result of public and media scrutiny. The sports world closely follows the draft process, dissecting the strengths and weaknesses of potential picks and engaging in spirited debates about who should be chosen first. These discussions generate immense hype and anticipation, building a narrative around the chosen player and fueling the expectations placed upon their shoulders.

For the players themselves, being selected as the number 1 draft pick can be both a dream come true and a double-edged sword. On one hand, it validates their hard work, talent, and dedication, affirming that they have reached the pinnacle of their sport. It offers them a platform to showcase their skills on the grandest stage and sets them on a trajectory that promises wealth, fame, and recognition.

On the other hand, the pressure to live up to the lofty expectations can be overwhelming. The spotlight shines brightly on these young athletes, magnifying every success and failure. Their performances are constantly scrutinized, and any perceived shortcomings or underwhelming moments are met with criticism and disappointment. The burden of carrying a franchise's hopes and the weight of the fans' expectations can take a toll on the mental and emotional well-being of these players.

The significance of number 1 draft picks goes beyond individual careers; it has a ripple effect on the league as a whole. Their success or failure can shape the narrative of a particular draft class, influencing the perception of that era and leaving a lasting impact on future drafts. The stories of those who faltered as number 1 draft picks serve as cautionary tales, reminding us that talent alone is not enough to guarantee success in the unforgiving world of professional sports.

In "Fallen Stars," we aim to explore the dichotomy between the immense promise and potential of number 1 draft picks and the stark reality faced by many of these individuals. Through the stories of LaRue Martin, Joe Barry Carroll, Austin Carr, Fred Hetzel, Tom Burleson, and others, we uncover the struggles, challenges, and external factors that contributed to their inability to meet the expectations placed upon them.

By examining the significance of number 1 draft picks and the weight of expectations, we hope to provide readers with a deeper understanding of the complexities involved in professional basketball. The journeys of these fallen stars serve as a reminder that greatness cannot be predetermined by draft position alone, and that the true measure of success extends beyond on-court accomplishments.

Join us as we delve into the stories of these troubled number 1 draft picks, uncovering the emotional toll, the shattered dreams, and the enduring legacies that shaped an era in the NBA. Through their experiences, we aim to challenge preconceived notions and foster a thoughtful reflection on the nature of success, resilience, and the human element in professional sports.

Historical context of the NBA during 1960-1980

To fully understand the stories and struggles of the troubled number 1 draft picks from 1960 to 1980, it is essential to explore the historical context in which they emerged. This period marked a transformative era in the NBA, characterized by societal changes, league expansion, and the rise of iconic players who left an indelible mark on the sport.

The 1960s and 1970s witnessed significant shifts in American society, with the civil rights movement, the Vietnam War, and cultural revolutions shaping the fabric of the nation. Against this backdrop, the NBA was undergoing its own evolution, striving to establish its place as a major professional sports league in the United States.

During this time, the NBA faced various challenges, including low television ratings, financial struggles, and limited exposure. However, it was also a period of growth and innovation. The league expanded from nine teams in 1960 to 22 teams by 1980, broadening its reach and attracting new fans. The NBA also witnessed the emergence of charismatic superstars such as Bill Russell, Wilt Chamberlain, Jerry West, Oscar Robertson, and Kareem Abdul-Jabbar, who captivated audiences with their exceptional skills and captivating personalities.

In terms of gameplay, the era was defined by a transition from a slow-paced, defensive-oriented style to a more up-tempo and high-scoring game. The introduction of the 24-second shot clock in 1954 had a profound impact on the sport, encouraging teams to play with greater speed and offensive efficiency. This change led to more dynamic and entertaining basketball, capturing the attention of fans and contributing to the growing popularity of the sport.

The NBA's cultural relevance and influence expanded during the 1960s and 1970s. The league embraced the counterculture movements of the era, with players expressing themselves through their fashion, hairstyles, and political activism. The NBA became a platform for athletes to voice their opinions and advocate for social change, reflecting the broader social movements of the time.

Against this backdrop of societal and cultural change, the number 1 draft picks from 1960 to 1980 entered the NBA with high expectations and aspirations. They represented the hopes and dreams of their respective teams and carried the weight of fan anticipation. However, they also faced unique challenges within the evolving landscape of professional basketball.

The NBA draft itself underwent several transformations during this period. Prior to 1966, the draft operated under a territorial pick system, allowing teams to select players from a designated geographic area without competition. However, the system was phased out in favor of a more egalitarian structure, wherein teams participated in a lottery to determine their draft order. This change aimed to ensure fairness and equality among the teams, and it had a profound impact on the dynamics of draft selections.

In addition to changes in the draft system, the NBA also experienced a shift in power dynamics between players and teams. The rise of free agency in the mid-1970s granted players more control over their careers, allowing them to negotiate contracts and seek opportunities with different teams. This newfound freedom provided players with greater agency but also introduced additional pressures and expectations in terms of performance and marketability.

It is within this historical context that the stories of LaRue Martin, Joe Barry Carroll, Austin Carr, Fred Hetzel, Tom Burleson, and others unfold. By understanding the cultural, social, and sporting landscape of the NBA during 1960-1980, we gain deeper insights into the challenges faced by these fallen stars and the factors that influenced their careers.

"Fallen Stars: The Untold Stories of Troubled Number 1 Draft Picks (1960-1980)" invites readers to journey through this transformative era, exploring the intersection of basketball, culture, and society. By contextualizing the experiences of these number 1 draft picks, we aim to provide a comprehensive understanding of the forces at play and shed light on the unique pressures and opportunities that shaped their careers. Through this exploration, we seek to unravel the captivating narratives of these fallen stars and offer a nuanced perspective on the troubled legacies that continue to resonate in the annals of professional basketball history.

Chapter 1: LaRue Martin, picked in 1972, retired in 1976

Early life and rise to basketball prominence

LaRue Martin, a name that resonated with hope and promise, was thrust into the spotlight when he became the number 1 draft pick in the 1972 NBA Draft. But before we delve into his professional career and the struggles he faced, it is essential to explore LaRue Martin's early life and his path to basketball prominence.

LaRue Martin was born on March 30, 1950, in Chicago, Illinois. Growing up in a city known for its rich basketball culture, Martin was introduced to the sport at a young age. As a child, he discovered a passion for basketball and displayed exceptional talent on the court. He honed his skills through countless hours of practice and competed against local players, carving out a reputation as one of Chicago's most promising young talents.

Martin attended De La Salle Institute, a renowned high school known for its strong basketball program. It was here that he truly began to make a name for himself. Standing at an impressive 6 feet 11 inches tall, Martin possessed a combination of size, agility, and skill that set him apart from his peers. His dominance in high school basketball caught the attention of college recruiters across the country.

Martin's outstanding performances garnered him numerous scholarship offers, but he ultimately chose to attend Loyola University in Chicago. Loyola presented an opportunity for Martin to stay close to home while also competing in a highly competitive basketball conference. As a member of the Loyola Ramblers, Martin continued to excel on the court, establishing himself as a force to be reckoned with in college basketball.

During his time at Loyola, Martin's skills as a center blossomed. He showcased impressive scoring ability, rebounding prowess, and shot-blocking skills, earning him recognition as one of the top collegiate players in the country. His dominant performances caught the attention of scouts and NBA executives, who began to take note of his potential as a future professional player.

Martin's rise to basketball prominence culminated in the 1972 NBA Draft. The Portland Trail Blazers held the coveted number 1 pick and ultimately selected Martin, pinning their hopes on the towering center to become a franchise cornerstone. The excitement and anticipation surrounding Martin's selection were palpable, with fans and analysts eagerly awaiting his NBA debut.

The decision to draft LaRue Martin ahead of other notable players in the draft class, including Bob McAdoo and Julius Erving, raised expectations to unprecedented heights. The Trail Blazers believed that Martin's combination of size, athleticism, and skill would be instrumental in transforming their struggling franchise into a contender. Martin was heralded as the savior of a team desperately in need of a turnaround.

As LaRue Martin embarked on his professional career, the weight of expectations bore heavily on his young shoulders. The transition from college to the NBA presented its own set of challenges. The level of competition escalated, and Martin found himself facing off against seasoned veterans and established stars. The intensity of the NBA game, both physically and mentally, posed a new test for the young center.

In the next chapter, we will explore the anticipation surrounding LaRue Martin's selection as the number 1 pick and the initial struggles and challenges he faced in the NBA. We will delve into the pressures and obstacles that awaited him as he sought to fulfill the lofty expectations placed upon him. Through the lens of LaRue Martin's story, we will gain valuable insights into the fragile nature of success and the complexities of professional basketball.

The anticipation surrounding his selection as the number 1 pick

In the spring of 1972, the Portland Trail Blazers held the esteemed honor of possessing the number 1 pick in the NBA Draft. This coveted position offered them the opportunity to select the player who would be the cornerstone of their franchise, a player who could potentially transform the struggling team into a championship contender. The anticipation surrounding the Trail Blazers' selection as the number 1 pick was palpable, and all eyes turned to the young center from Loyola University, LaRue Martin.

As the draft approached, the buzz surrounding LaRue Martin grew exponentially. His impressive performances in college, coupled with his imposing 6 feet 11 inches frame, made him an intriguing prospect for NBA teams. The media and basketball analysts speculated on the potential impact Martin could have in the professional ranks, fueling the anticipation surrounding his selection.

The Trail Blazers' decision to choose LaRue Martin as the number 1 pick in the 1972 NBA Draft was met with a mix of excitement, optimism, and skepticism. Fans and experts debated whether Martin was truly deserving of the top selection, especially when other notable players like Bob

McAdoo and Julius Erving were available in the draft class. The pressure on Martin to live up to the expectations of being the first pick was immense, with many expecting him to lead the franchise to newfound success.

The anticipation surrounding Martin's selection extended beyond the Trail Blazers organization. NBA fans across the country were eager to witness the debut of the highly-touted center. The media followed Martin closely, speculating on how his skills and attributes would translate to the professional level. There was a sense of curiosity and excitement about the potential impact he could have on the league.

For LaRue Martin himself, the anticipation was both exhilarating and daunting. The opportunity to play in the NBA was a dream come true, but the weight of expectations was a heavy burden to bear. Martin understood the significance of being the number 1 pick and the responsibility that came with it. He was determined to prove his worth and justify the Trail Blazers' faith in him.

The anticipation surrounding Martin's selection reached its peak on October 10, 1972, when he made his NBA debut. As he stepped onto the court for his first professional game, the spotlight was firmly on him. Fans eagerly awaited his every move, analyzing his performance with scrutiny. The pressure to perform and validate his selection as the number 1 pick was immense.

In the early stages of his NBA career, Martin showed glimpses of his potential. He displayed his scoring ability, rebounding prowess, and shot-blocking skills, giving fans a taste of what he was capable of achieving. However, as the season progressed, it became clear that Martin was facing challenges in adapting to the rigors of the NBA. He struggled with consistency and faced difficulties in asserting his dominance against more experienced opponents.

The disparity between the lofty expectations placed upon LaRue Martin and the reality of his performance created a sense of disappointment among fans and critics. The initial excitement surrounding his selection began to wane as doubts emerged about his ability to live up to the hype. The scrutiny intensified, putting even more pressure on Martin to prove himself and silence his detractors.

In the next section, we will explore the initial struggles and challenges that LaRue Martin faced in the NBA. We will delve into the factors that contributed to his difficulties in meeting the sky-high expectations placed upon him. Through the lens of Martin's story, we will gain a deeper understanding of the challenges that young players face when stepping into the spotlight as the number 1 draft pick.

Initial struggles and challenges faced in the NBA

LaRue Martin's journey in the NBA began with immense anticipation and high expectations. As the number 1 draft pick in the 1972 NBA Draft, he was hailed as the savior of the Portland Trail Blazers, a team desperately in need of a turnaround. However, the transition from college to the professional ranks presented Martin with a set of challenges that would test his mettle and resilience.

One of the initial struggles LaRue Martin faced in the NBA was the steep learning curve. The level of competition in the professional league was significantly higher than what he had encountered in college. He was now facing off against seasoned veterans and established stars who possessed a wealth of experience and knowledge about the game. Adjusting to the speed, physicality, and tactical nuances of the NBA proved to be a formidable task for the young center.

Martin's lack of NBA experience also meant that he had to adapt to a different style of play. In college, he had thrived as a dominant force in the paint, utilizing his size and athleticism to overpower opponents. However, in the NBA, Martin found himself facing stronger and more skilled opponents who were adept at neutralizing his strengths. He had to refine his offensive repertoire, develop new strategies, and find ways to contribute to his team's success in a more nuanced manner.

Additionally, Martin faced the challenge of playing for a struggling franchise. The Portland Trail Blazers were in the midst of a rebuilding phase when he joined the team. They lacked the necessary supporting cast and infrastructure to maximize his potential and provide him with the necessary guidance and mentorship. Martin was thrust into a situation where he was expected to single-handedly transform the team's fortunes, adding an extra layer of pressure to his already demanding rookie season.

The weight of expectations placed upon LaRue Martin was another significant challenge he had to confront. Being the number 1 draft pick came with lofty assumptions and a spotlight that followed his every move. Fans, media, and the organization had invested so much hope in his success that anything less than immediate excellence was deemed a disappointment. The pressure to live up to these sky-high expectations was immense and could have a profound psychological impact on a young player's confidence and performance.

Martin also encountered obstacles in adjusting to the lifestyle and demands of being an NBA player. The grueling schedule, constant travel, and the scrutiny that came with fame and fortune presented their own set of challenges. Balancing the demands of a professional basketball career with personal life and maintaining physical and mental well-being proved to be an ongoing struggle for Martin.

Amidst these challenges, LaRue Martin persevered and sought to improve his game. He dedicated countless hours to practice, honing his skills, and refining his understanding of the NBA. He sought guidance from coaches, teammates, and veterans in an attempt to accelerate his development and bridge the gap between his potential and his performance.

Despite his efforts, Martin's struggles persisted throughout his NBA career. His on-court performances failed to meet the lofty expectations set for him, leading to growing criticism and doubt. The disappointment surrounding his perceived underachievement only intensified as time went on, further exacerbating the challenges he faced.

In the next section, we will explore LaRue Martin's failed attempts at redemption and the eventual decision to retire. We will delve into the factors that contributed to his inability to live up to the expectations placed upon him and the emotional toll it took on his career. Through Martin's story, we will gain a deeper understanding of the complexities and pressures faced by number 1 draft picks in the NBA.

Failed attempts at redemption and eventual retirement

LaRue Martin's NBA career was marked by struggles and unfulfilled potential. Despite the initial excitement surrounding his selection as the number 1 pick in the 1972 NBA Draft, Martin found it difficult to live up to the expectations placed upon him. As the seasons passed, he made several attempts at redemption, but ultimately, the weight of his underperformance and the psychological toll it took on him led to his decision to retire from professional basketball.

After a disappointing rookie season, Martin recognized the need to improve and make adjustments to his game. He worked tirelessly in the offseason, focusing on refining his skills, strengthening his body, and enhancing his basketball IQ. The following season, he hoped to show significant progress and prove his critics wrong.

However, despite his efforts, Martin continued to struggle on the court. His performances remained inconsistent, and he failed to establish himself as a dominant force in the league. The scrutiny and criticism surrounding his underachievement only intensified, further eroding his confidence and affecting his mental state.

Martin's failed attempts at redemption were also influenced by external factors beyond his control. The lack of a strong supporting cast and a cohesive team system hindered his ability to flourish. The Trail Blazers, as a franchise, were grappling with organizational issues and were unable to provide the necessary stability and structure for Martin's development. The constant changes in coaching staff and roster instability further impeded his progress.

Additionally, injuries plagued Martin throughout his NBA career, adding another layer of adversity to his already challenging journey. These physical setbacks limited his playing time and hindered his ability to establish a consistent rhythm on the court. The injuries not only affected his performance but also took a toll on his mental and emotional well-being, as he faced the frustration and disappointment of being unable to fully showcase his abilities.

The cumulative effect of these challenges gradually wore down LaRue Martin's passion and motivation for the game. The immense pressure and the inability to meet the expectations placed upon him took a significant toll on his confidence and self-belief. As the seasons went by, Martin's desire to prove himself waned, and he found it increasingly difficult to find joy in playing basketball.

Ultimately, after four seasons in the NBA, LaRue Martin made the difficult decision to retire from professional basketball in 1976. His retirement marked the end of a tumultuous journey that began with high hopes and ended in unfulfilled potential. The decision to step away from the game was a deeply personal one, driven by a combination of factors, including the mental and emotional toll of his struggles, the frustration of not reaching his expected level of success, and the realization that it was time to move on to a new chapter in his life.

LaRue Martin's retirement from the NBA was not the ending he or others had envisioned when he was drafted as the number 1 pick. It was a moment of reflection and introspection, as he grappled with the weight of unfulfilled expectations and the questions of what could have been. However, his legacy as a fallen star serves as a reminder of the fragility of success and the unpredictable nature of professional sports.

In the next chapter, we will explore the life after retirement for LaRue Martin and the challenges he faced in transitioning to a post-NBA career. We will delve into the emotional and psychological impact of his basketball journey, and the lessons that can be learned from his story. Through Martin's experiences, we will gain a deeper understanding of the complexities of professional sports and the profound effects they can have on athletes' lives.

Chapter 2: Joe Barry Carroll, picked in 1980, retired in 1991

Background and college success leading to high expectations

Joe Barry Carroll's journey in basketball began with tremendous promise and high expectations. With an impressive college career and a standout performance at Purdue University, Carroll emerged as one of the most highly touted prospects in the 1980 NBA Draft. In this section, we will explore Carroll's background and the college success that set the stage for the heightened expectations surrounding his selection as the number 1 pick.

Born on July 24, 1958, in Pine Bluff, Arkansas, Joe Barry Carroll displayed an early affinity for basketball. He excelled as a young athlete, showcasing exceptional size, agility, and skills on the court. Carroll's physical attributes, combined with his natural talent and work ethic, caught the attention of college recruiters across the country.

Carroll's collegiate journey began when he joined the Purdue Boilermakers in 1976. Under the guidance of head coach Fred Schaus, Carroll quickly established himself as a force to be reckoned with. Standing at 7 feet tall, he possessed an impressive wingspan and a versatile skill set that allowed him to dominate both offensively and defensively.

During his time at Purdue, Carroll showcased his scoring prowess and ability to impact the game on multiple fronts. He became known for his smooth shooting stroke, scoring touch around the rim, and solid rebounding skills. Carroll's offensive versatility, which included a reliable mid-range jumper and an effective post-up game, made him a difficult matchup for opposing teams.

In his sophomore season, Carroll led the Boilermakers to an impressive run in the NCAA Tournament, displaying his ability to perform on the big stage. This success continued into his junior and senior years, where he consistently put up impressive numbers and earned accolades for his performances. Carroll's impact on the college basketball landscape was undeniable, and he emerged as a highly regarded prospect heading into the NBA Draft.

The combination of Carroll's dominant college career, his physical attributes, and his basketball skills elevated the expectations surrounding his NBA future. As the 1980 NBA Draft approached, he was widely touted as a potential franchise-altering talent. NBA teams were hopeful that Carroll could provide an immediate impact, with his scoring ability and defensive presence, and potentially lead their respective organizations to success.

Carroll's selection as the number 1 pick in the 1980 NBA Draft by the Golden State Warriors only intensified the anticipation surrounding his professional debut. The Warriors, a franchise in need of a turnaround, saw in Carroll the potential to revitalize their team and bring them back to relevance. Fans, media, and the organization placed their hopes on Carroll's broad shoulders, expecting him to be a transformative figure and a cornerstone for future success.

The high expectations placed upon Joe Barry Carroll were not only a product of his college success but also a reflection of the broader cultural and societal context of the time. The 1980s marked a period of transition in the NBA, as the league was on the verge of a new era of popularity and global recognition. The emergence of television coverage and the increasing global interest in basketball elevated the significance of top draft picks, making them symbols of hope and potential greatness.

As Carroll prepared to embark on his NBA career, the weight of these expectations loomed large. The transition from the college game to the professional ranks presented its own set of challenges, and Carroll would soon discover that the road to fulfilling those lofty expectations would not be without its obstacles.

In the next section, we will delve into the pressure of living up to the number 1 pick status and the impact it had on Joe Barry Carroll's career. We will explore how external factors and the weight of expectations influenced his performance and shaped his professional journey. Through Carroll's story, we gain insight into the complexities of the NBA landscape and the challenges faced by highly anticipated rookies in their quest to meet or exceed the expectations placed upon them.

The pressure of living up to the number 1 pick status

Joe Barry Carroll entered the NBA with the weight of enormous expectations on his shoulders. As the number 1 pick in the 1980 NBA Draft, Carroll was tasked with living up to the hype and fulfilling the hopes of the Golden State Warriors organization and their fans. In this section, we will explore the immense pressure Carroll faced as a top draft pick and the impact it had on his career.

Being selected as the number 1 pick in any professional sports draft carries with it a set of unique challenges. The player becomes a symbol of hope and potential, representing the future of the franchise. The pressure to perform at a high level from the outset can be overwhelming, and Joe Barry Carroll was no exception.

The Golden State Warriors had pinned their hopes on Carroll to be a transformative player who could lead them back to contention. The expectations placed on him were sky-high, with fans and media eagerly anticipating his impact on the team's success. Carroll was expected to be the face of the franchise, a player who could elevate the Warriors to new heights.

The pressure to live up to the number 1 pick status affected Carroll both on and off the court. He faced scrutiny from fans, media, and his own teammates, all of whom had high expectations for his performance. Every move he made, every shot he took, was heavily scrutinized and analyzed. The pressure to succeed became a constant presence in his basketball career.

Carroll's struggles to meet these expectations were not solely due to a lack of talent or effort. The transition from college to the NBA is a significant leap, and it often takes time for players to adjust to the faster pace, physicality, and overall level of competition. The steep learning curve combined with the pressure of being a top draft pick created a challenging environment for Carroll to thrive in.

Additionally, Carroll's playing style and demeanor contributed to the perception of him not living up to expectations. His smooth, effortless playing style led some to interpret his on-court demeanor as lackadaisical or disengaged. This perception further fueled the criticism surrounding his performance and added to the mounting pressure he faced.

The pressure of living up to the number 1 pick status also affected Carroll's confidence and mental state. The constant scrutiny and criticism took a toll on his self-belief, causing him to question his abilities and second-guess his decisions on the court. The fear of failure and the weight of expectations can be paralyzing, leading to hesitancy and a lack of assertiveness in one's game.

Furthermore, Carroll's struggles were exacerbated by the lack of a strong supporting cast and stability within the Warriors organization during his early years. The team underwent coaching changes, front office turmoil, and roster turnover, making it difficult for Carroll to find his footing and build chemistry with his teammates. These external factors added another layer of pressure and hindered his ability to fully showcase his talents.

Despite these challenges, Carroll did have moments of success during his NBA career. He displayed flashes of brilliance, showcasing his scoring ability and versatility on the court. However, the inconsistencies in his performance and the inability to consistently meet the lofty expectations led to frustration and disappointment for himself and those around him.

The pressure of living up to the number 1 pick status is a burden that many highly touted rookies in the NBA have experienced. It is a double-edged sword, as the same expectations that drive players to excel can also become a source of immense pressure and hinder their development. It requires not only exceptional talent but also mental fortitude and resilience to navigate the challenges and expectations that come with being a top draft pick.

In the next section, we will delve into the promising moments and underwhelming performances of Joe Barry Carroll's career. We will explore the factors that contributed to his struggles and examine the impact of off-court factors on his trajectory in the NBA. Through Carroll's story, we gain insight into the complexities of navigating the pressures and expectations of being a number 1 draft pick.

Promising moments and underwhelming performances

Joe Barry Carroll's NBA career was a mixture of promising moments and underwhelming performances. While he showed flashes of brilliance and undeniable talent, his overall impact fell short of the lofty expectations placed upon him as the number 1 draft pick. In this section, we will explore the highs and lows of Carroll's career, examining the moments that showcased his potential and the factors that contributed to his underwhelming performances.

Carroll's rookie season in the NBA provided glimpses of his immense talent and potential. He averaged 18.9 points and 9.3 rebounds per game, showcasing his scoring ability and versatility as a big man. His size, shooting touch, and post-up skills made him a difficult matchup for opponents. Carroll's performance earned him a spot on the NBA All-Rookie First Team, solidifying his status as a rising star in the league.

The following season, Carroll continued to make strides in his game, averaging 22.7 points per game and further establishing himself as a scoring threat. His offensive repertoire expanded, and he displayed improved shot selection and efficiency. Carroll's success on the court provided hope that he was on the path to fulfilling the expectations placed upon him.

However, as Carroll's career progressed, inconsistencies in his performance became more apparent. He struggled with maintaining a high level of play consistently, often following strong performances with lackluster ones. These inconsistencies raised questions about his ability to deliver on a nightly basis and added to the frustrations of fans and the organization.

One factor that contributed to Carroll's underwhelming performances was his perceived lack of aggressiveness and assertiveness on the court. Despite possessing the physical tools and skills to dominate, there were instances where Carroll seemed passive or disengaged during games. This passivity hindered his impact and left observers yearning for more consistency and intensity from the talented big man.

Furthermore, Carroll's defensive presence did not match his offensive capabilities. While he had the potential to be a dominant force on both ends of the court, his defensive contributions often fell short. Inconsistencies in his effort and positioning on defense were evident, limiting his overall impact and raising concerns about his commitment to the game.

Off-court factors also played a role in Carroll's underwhelming performances. The pressures and distractions that come with being a professional athlete, coupled with personal challenges and external influences, affected his focus and dedication to the game. Carroll faced criticism for his lifestyle choices, and reports of clashes with teammates and coaches further clouded his reputation.

Additionally, the instability within the Warriors organization during Carroll's tenure impacted his development and performance. Frequent coaching changes, front office turmoil, and roster turnover disrupted the team's chemistry and hindered Carroll's ability to build meaningful connections with his teammates. The lack of stability and continuity made it difficult for Carroll to thrive and find his place within the organization.

Despite the inconsistencies and underwhelming performances, Carroll did have notable moments throughout his career that showcased his potential. He had several high-scoring games and memorable performances, reminding everyone of his scoring prowess and offensive skill set. These glimpses of brilliance provided a tantalizing reminder of the talent that Carroll possessed.

In the next section, we will examine the impact of off-court factors on Joe Barry Carroll's career trajectory. We will delve into the personal challenges and external influences that affected his focus, dedication, and overall performance on the basketball court. By understanding the broader context of Carroll's journey, we can gain a deeper appreciation for the complexities of an NBA player's life and the factors that can shape their career.

The impact of off-court factors on his career trajectory

Joe Barry Carroll's NBA career was not only shaped by his on-court performances but also by a range of off-court factors that influenced his trajectory in the league. In this section, we will explore the impact of these off-court factors on Carroll's career, including personal challenges, external influences, and the overall context of his life during his time in the NBA.

One significant off-court factor that affected Carroll's career was the scrutiny and criticism he faced for his lifestyle choices. Throughout his time in the NBA, Carroll was known for his extravagant and flamboyant personality. He embraced the glamorous side of being a professional athlete, which sometimes led to negative perceptions from fans, media, and even within his own organization. The attention focused on his off-court activities sometimes overshadowed his on-court performances and created distractions that impacted his focus and dedication to the game.

Carroll's personal life also had its share of challenges that influenced his career. Like many young athletes thrust into the spotlight, he had to navigate the pressures and temptations that come with fame and fortune. These personal challenges, including maintaining relationships, managing finances, and dealing with the demands of the NBA lifestyle, could have affected his mindset and focus on basketball.

In addition to personal challenges, external influences played a role in Carroll's career trajectory. The media's portrayal of him as a talented player who didn't fully live up to expectations added to the pressure and scrutiny he faced. Negative narratives and criticisms can impact an athlete's confidence and contribute to a sense of underachievement. It is important to recognize that the media's portrayal of Carroll's career was not the sole determinant of his performance, but it did shape public perception and potentially influenced how he was perceived within NBA circles.

The instability within the Golden State Warriors organization during Carroll's tenure also impacted his career. The team underwent multiple coaching changes, front office turmoil, and roster turnover, creating an environment of uncertainty and inconsistency. These organizational challenges made it difficult for Carroll to establish a stable support system and build strong relationships with coaches and teammates. The lack of stability and continuity hindered his development and prevented him from reaching his full potential.

Furthermore, the broader social and cultural context of the NBA during Carroll's era played a role in shaping his career. The 1980s were marked by a unique blend of basketball and popular culture, with the emergence of superstars like Magic Johnson, Larry Bird, and Michael Jordan. Carroll had to compete in an era where the expectations for success were high, and the competition was fierce. The dominance of other players and teams during this era may have contributed to the perception that Carroll fell short of expectations.

It is important to note that while off-court factors undoubtedly had an impact on Carroll's career, they do not absolve him of personal responsibility. Professional athletes must make choices and sacrifices to succeed at the highest level, and Carroll's career trajectory can be viewed as a combination of both external influences and personal decisions.

In the next section, we will explore the underwhelming moments of Carroll's career and examine the factors that contributed to his struggles. We will delve into the challenges he faced on the court and the impact they had on his overall performance. By examining the full context of Carroll's career, we can gain a deeper understanding of the complexities and challenges faced by highly touted athletes in the NBA.

Chapter 3: Austin Carr, picked in 1971, retired in 1981

Collegiate stardom and high hopes as a number 1 draft pick

Austin Carr's journey to the NBA as the number 1 draft pick in 1971 was fueled by his collegiate stardom and the high expectations placed upon him. In this section, we will explore Carr's impressive college career, his rise to prominence, and the immense anticipation surrounding his selection as the top pick in the NBA draft.

Carr's basketball journey began in Washington, D.C., where he attended Mackin Catholic High School. Even at the high school level, Carr displayed exceptional talent and was recognized as one of the top players in the region. His scoring ability, athleticism, and basketball instincts made him a highly sought-after prospect by college programs across the country.

Ultimately, Carr chose to attend the University of Notre Dame, where he would leave an indelible mark on the college basketball landscape. As a freshman, Carr burst onto the scene, averaging an impressive 38.1 points per game, leading the nation in scoring. His scoring prowess, combined with his smooth shooting stroke and ability to create his own shot, made him a nightmare for opposing defenses.

Carr's stellar play continued throughout his college career, earning him the nickname "Mr. Notre Dame" and solidifying his status as one of the greatest players in the history of the university. He became the all-time leading scorer at Notre Dame, finishing his collegiate career with an impressive 2,560 points. Carr's impact extended beyond his individual statistics; he brought national attention and recognition to the Notre Dame basketball program.

As Carr's college career progressed, expectations for his NBA future grew. The anticipation surrounding his selection as the number 1 draft pick in 1971 was immense. NBA teams and fans envisioned Carr as a transformative player who could elevate a franchise to new heights. The combination of his college success, natural talent, and charismatic personality made him a highly marketable prospect.

When the Cleveland Cavaliers selected Carr with the first pick in the 1971 NBA draft, the city of Cleveland embraced him as their basketball savior. The Cavaliers were a struggling franchise at the time, and Carr's arrival brought hope and excitement to the team and its fans. He was seen as the player who could revitalize the Cavaliers and turn them into a competitive force in the NBA.

The pressure of living up to the number 1 draft pick status weighed heavily on Carr's shoulders. The expectations were sky-high, and he faced the challenge of translating his college success to the professional level. Carr was expected to become a franchise cornerstone, leading the Cavaliers to success and becoming a perennial All-Star.

In his rookie season, Carr demonstrated flashes of brilliance, averaging 21.2 points per game and earning a spot on the NBA All-Rookie First Team. He showcased his scoring ability, smooth offensive game, and clutch performances that endeared him to Cavaliers fans. It seemed as though Carr was on the path to fulfilling the lofty expectations placed upon him.

However, injuries plagued Carr throughout his NBA career, derailing his progress and preventing him from reaching his full potential. He suffered several knee injuries that required surgeries and extensive rehabilitation. These injuries limited his mobility and explosiveness, hindering his ability to perform at his peak and impacting his overall effectiveness on the court.

Despite the setbacks, Carr remained resilient and displayed a remarkable determination to overcome adversity. He adjusted his game to compensate for his physical limitations and became a more intelligent and crafty player. Carr's basketball IQ and leadership qualities allowed him to remain a valuable contributor to the Cavaliers, even if he didn't reach the heights that were initially envisioned for him.

In the next section, we will explore the challenges and setbacks Carr faced in the NBA and how they influenced his career trajectory. We will examine the impact of injuries, changes in the Cavaliers' roster and coaching staff, and the emotional toll of unfulfilled expectations. Through Carr's story, we gain insight into the fragility of success and the resilience required to navigate the unpredictable journey of a professional basketball career.

Initial success and glimpses of potential in the NBA

After being selected as the number 1 draft pick in 1971 by the Cleveland Cavaliers, Austin Carr entered the NBA with high expectations. In this section, we will explore Carr's initial success and the glimpses of potential he showed during his early years in the league. We will delve into his rookie season, standout performances, and the promise he displayed as a young player.

Carr's transition to the NBA was met with a wave of enthusiasm from both the Cavaliers organization and their fans. With his collegiate stardom and dynamic scoring ability, he was seen as a player who could transform the struggling franchise into a competitive force. The pressure to live up to the number 1 draft pick status was immense, but Carr embraced the challenge and set out to make his mark in the NBA.

In his rookie season, Carr wasted no time in demonstrating his scoring prowess and offensive skills. He made an immediate impact, averaging 21.2 points per game, which was the highest among all rookies that year. Carr's ability to create his own shot, navigate through defenses, and score from various spots on the court made him a difficult player to guard. His smooth shooting stroke and natural scoring instincts were on full display, captivating fans and earning him the nickname "Mr. Cavalier."

One of the defining moments of Carr's rookie season came on February 21, 1972, when he exploded for a historic performance against the Portland Trail Blazers. In that game, Carr poured in an astonishing 44 points, setting a new NBA record for most points scored by a rookie in a single game. His offensive outburst showcased his ability to take over a game and solidified his status as one of the league's most exciting young talents.

Carr's scoring prowess wasn't limited to individual games. He consistently put up impressive numbers throughout his early years in the NBA. In the 1973-74 season, he averaged 21.9 points per game, establishing himself as one of the league's premier scorers. Carr's offensive repertoire included an array of moves, including mid-range jumpers, floaters, and acrobatic finishes at the rim. His scoring ability made him a fan favorite and drew comparisons to some of the league's greatest players.

Beyond his scoring ability, Carr also showcased versatility and all-around skills. He displayed court vision and passing ability, often finding open teammates with pinpoint assists. His basketball IQ allowed him to make smart decisions on the court and contribute in various facets of the game. Carr's well-rounded skills and offensive prowess made him a formidable force and a player with tremendous potential.

During his early years in the league, Carr's performances garnered recognition and accolades. He was selected as an NBA All-Star in both the 1973-74 and 1974-75 seasons, solidifying his status among the league's elite players. His inclusion in the All-Star game was a testament to his impact on the court and the respect he garnered from coaches, players, and fans.

While Carr's initial success and glimpses of potential were undeniable, they were not without challenges. Injuries, roster changes, and other external factors would present obstacles that Carr would need to overcome in order to sustain his success and reach his full potential. These challenges, which we will explore in the following sections, would shape Carr's NBA journey and contribute to the complexities of his career.

In the next section, we will examine the setbacks and obstacles that Carr faced in his NBA career, including the impact of injuries and changes within the Cavaliers' organization. By understanding the challenges Carr encountered, we can gain insight into the factors that shaped his career trajectory and the subsequent struggles he faced.

Injuries and setbacks derailing his progress

Despite Austin Carr's initial success and glimpses of potential in the NBA, his career was plagued by injuries and setbacks that derailed his progress. In this section, we will explore the various injuries Carr endured throughout his career and how they impacted his development as a player. We will also examine the setbacks he faced within the Cleveland Cavaliers organization and the challenges of maintaining consistency and reaching his full potential.

Carr's first major setback came during his third season in the NBA when he suffered a significant foot injury. The injury required surgery and forced him to miss a considerable portion of the 1973-74 season. The absence of Carr, the team's leading scorer, had a profound impact on the Cavaliers' performance. Without his scoring and leadership on the court, the team struggled to maintain their competitive edge and suffered a decline in their overall record.

The foot injury marked the beginning of a series of physical challenges for Carr. Throughout his career, he would battle a myriad of injuries, including knee and ankle issues, which would hinder his ability to perform at his peak. These injuries not only affected his mobility and explosiveness but also limited his playing time and disrupted his rhythm on the court. The recurring nature of these injuries prevented Carr from reaching his full potential and having a consistent impact on the game.

In addition to the physical setbacks, Carr also faced challenges within the Cavaliers organization. The team underwent changes in coaching staff and roster composition, which had an impact on Carr's role and opportunities. Coaching philosophies and strategies differed, and the adjustments required Carr to adapt to new systems and playing styles. These changes often disrupted the continuity and chemistry of the team, making it difficult for Carr to find his rhythm and establish a stable foundation for success.

Furthermore, the Cavaliers experienced a lack of overall success during Carr's tenure, struggling to make significant progress in the highly competitive NBA landscape. The team faced difficulties in assembling a strong supporting cast around Carr, which limited their ability to contend for championships. The absence of consistent success and the pressure to carry the team's offensive load took a toll on Carr both physically and mentally.

Despite the setbacks, Carr continued to display resilience and determination. He underwent rigorous rehabilitation to recover from his injuries and returned to the court, showcasing his perseverance and love for the game. Carr's passion and work ethic remained unwavering, even in the face of adversity.

However, the cumulative effects of injuries and setbacks gradually took a toll on Carr's overall performance. As his athleticism and explosiveness diminished, he had to rely more on his basketball IQ and experience to contribute to the team. While he was still able to provide valuable contributions, his impact on the court was not as prominent as it had been earlier in his career.

The combination of injuries, organizational challenges, and the wear and tear of a long NBA career eventually led to Carr's decision to retire in 1981. The decision to step away from the game marked the end of a career that had been marked by both triumphs and hardships.

In the next section, we will explore Carr's life after retirement and how he navigated the transition from being a professional basketball player to the next phase of his life. We will examine the challenges he faced and the contributions he made off the court, as well as his enduring legacy in the basketball community.

Coping with unfulfilled expectations and life after retirement

After Austin Carr retired from professional basketball in 1981, he faced the challenge of coping with unfulfilled expectations and transitioning to life after his playing career. In this section, we will explore the emotional journey Carr experienced as he grappled with the highs and lows of his NBA career. We will also examine how he navigated the transition to a new chapter in his life and the contributions he made off the court.

The end of Carr's playing career marked a period of reflection and introspection. Despite his early success and the promise he showed as the number 1 draft pick, Carr's NBA career hadn't unfolded as many had anticipated. The unfulfilled expectations and the gap between his potential and the reality of his career weighed heavily on Carr's mind. He had to come to terms with the fact that his playing days were over and reconcile his own self-perception with the external perceptions of his basketball career.

Carr faced the challenge of finding a new purpose and identity beyond basketball. For many professional athletes, the transition from the spotlight of the court to the anonymity of everyday life can be daunting. Carr had to redefine himself and discover new passions and pursuits that would bring fulfillment and a sense of purpose. This transition wasn't easy, but Carr's resilience and determination allowed him to navigate this period of adjustment.

One avenue Carr explored was a career in broadcasting. Recognizing his deep knowledge of the game and his ability to articulate his insights, Carr became a color commentator for NBA games. Through his broadcasting work, he was able to stay connected to the sport he loved and share his experiences and expertise with fans. Carr's charismatic personality and engaging commentary endeared him to audiences, further solidifying his place in the basketball community.

Off the court, Carr also dedicated himself to various philanthropic endeavors. He established the Austin Carr Scholarship Foundation, which aimed to provide educational opportunities for underprivileged students. Through his foundation, Carr sought to make a positive impact on the lives of young people, emphasizing the importance of education and the pursuit of dreams. His commitment to giving back to the community showcased his character and the values instilled in him throughout his basketball journey.

Carr's experiences and insights also led him to mentor young players and offer guidance to those navigating their own NBA careers. He understood the challenges and pressures that came with being a professional athlete, and he used his own experiences as lessons to help others. Carr's mentoring and support were invaluable to many young players, providing them with a trusted advisor who had experienced both the triumphs and tribulations of the game.

Coping with unfulfilled expectations required Carr to embrace a new perspective on success. While his NBA career may not have met the lofty expectations set for him, Carr came to understand that success can take many forms. He realized that his impact extended beyond the statistics and accolades, and that his legacy was not solely defined by his on-court performance. The resilience he showed in the face of adversity, his contributions off the court, and the positive influence he had on others were all measures of his true greatness.

In retrospect, Carr's journey serves as a reminder that success in life is not always a linear path. It is marked by ups and downs, triumphs and setbacks, and the ability to adapt and find purpose in new chapters. Carr's story is one of resilience, reinvention, and the enduring power of the human spirit.

In the next section, we will examine the broader themes and lessons that can be drawn from the experiences of Carr and other number 1 draft picks. We will analyze the commonalities and patterns among their stories and reflect on the true measure of greatness in professional basketball.

Chapter 4: Fred Hetzel, picked in 1965, retired in 1971

The story of Fred Hetzel's journey from college to the NBA

In this section, we will delve into the captivating story of Fred Hetzel, tracing his journey from college basketball stardom to his NBA career. We will explore the early years of Hetzel's life, his rise to prominence in college basketball, and the anticipation surrounding his selection as a number 1 draft pick. This chapter will shed light on the experiences and challenges that shaped Hetzel's path to the professional level.

1. Early Life and Introduction to Basketball

To understand Fred Hetzel's journey, we must start with his early life. Born on October 21, 1942, in Washington, D.C., Hetzel grew up with a passion for sports. Basketball quickly became his primary focus, and he honed his skills on neighborhood courts and high school teams. Hetzel's talent and work ethic soon caught the attention of college recruiters, setting the stage for his remarkable collegiate career.

2. Collegiate Stardom at Davidson College

Hetzel's basketball prowess led him to Davidson College, a small liberal arts school in North Carolina. Under the guidance of head coach Lefty Driesell, Hetzel flourished on the court. Known for his smooth shooting stroke and versatility, Hetzel became a dominant force in college basketball.

We will explore Hetzel's standout performances and achievements during his time at Davidson. From leading the Southern Conference in scoring to receiving All-American honors, Hetzel's impact on the college basketball landscape was undeniable. His success at Davidson earned him national recognition and set the stage for his transition to the NBA.

3. The Anticipation of Becoming a Number 1 Draft Pick

As Hetzel's college career drew to a close, the anticipation surrounding his future in the NBA grew. With his size, scoring ability, and basketball IQ, Hetzel was widely regarded as one of the top prospects in the 1965 NBA Draft. NBA scouts and general managers recognized his potential and envisioned him as a franchise player who could make an immediate impact at the professional level.

We will delve into the pre-draft process and the speculation surrounding Hetzel's potential landing spot. We will explore the expectations placed upon him as a number 1 draft pick and the pressure that accompanied such a lofty status. Hetzel's selection as the top pick in the draft marked the beginning of a new chapter in his basketball journey.

4. Transitioning to the NBA and Rookie Season

Hetzel's entry into the NBA came with its own set of challenges and adjustments. As a rookie, he faced the task of acclimating to the faster pace, physicality, and heightened competition of professional basketball. We will delve into Hetzel's experiences during his rookie season, including his interactions with veteran teammates, the demands of the NBA schedule, and the adjustments he had to make to his game.

5. Career Challenges and Personal Growth

While Hetzel showcased flashes of his potential in the NBA, his career faced numerous challenges. Injuries, roster changes, and coaching transitions impacted his development and playing time. We will examine the obstacles Hetzel encountered throughout his NBA career and how they shaped his trajectory.

Despite the challenges, Hetzel's time in the NBA provided opportunities for personal growth and resilience. We will explore how he navigated the highs and lows, and the lessons he learned along the way. Hetzel's character and perseverance in the face of adversity offer valuable insights into the realities of professional sports and the determination required to overcome obstacles.

6. Reflecting on a Career that Fell Short of Expectations

As Hetzel's NBA career came to a close, he had to come to terms with the gap between the expectations placed upon him and the realities of his playing career. We will explore Hetzel's reflections on his time in the NBA, the emotions he experienced when his career did not reach the heights predicted, and the impact this had on his personal and professional life.

We will also examine how Hetzel's career is remembered in retrospect. Does his legacy solely revolve around unfulfilled potential, or are there other aspects of his career that deserve recognition? By examining the perceptions of Hetzel's career, we can gain a deeper understanding of the complexities of evaluating athletes' legacies.

In this section, we will provide a comprehensive account of Fred Hetzel's journey from college basketball star to his NBA career. By exploring the key moments, challenges, and personal growth throughout his basketball career, we gain insights into the fragile nature of success and the impact it can have on an athlete's life. Hetzel's story serves as a poignant example of the pressures and expectations placed upon number 1 draft picks and the unique paths they navigate in pursuit of their dreams.

Struggles with injuries and inconsistency in the league

In this section, we will delve into the challenges that Fred Hetzel faced during his NBA career, focusing specifically on his struggles with injuries and inconsistency. Despite his immense talent and early success, Hetzel's path was marred by physical setbacks and difficulties finding consistent performance on the court. This chapter will shed light on the impact of injuries and the toll they took on Hetzel's career, as well as the factors contributing to his inconsistency.

1. The Initial Impact of Injuries

As Hetzel embarked on his NBA career, injuries quickly became a recurring theme. We will explore the early injuries that disrupted his rookie season and the subsequent impact they had on his confidence, playing time, and ability to establish a rhythm. By examining the specific injuries Hetzel faced and their consequences, we gain insights into the physical challenges he had to overcome.

2. The Mental and Emotional Toll

In addition to the physical pain and limitations caused by injuries, we will delve into the mental and emotional toll they took on Hetzel. Injuries often lead to frustration, doubt, and a loss of confidence, affecting an athlete's overall performance and mindset. We will explore Hetzel's mindset during these challenging times and the strategies he employed to cope with the psychological aspects of his injuries.

3. The Ripple Effect on Consistency

Hetzel's struggles with injuries had a direct impact on his consistency on the court. We will examine how the lack of consistent playing time and disrupted training regimens affected his ability to find a rhythm and perform at his best. The inconsistency in his performance can be traced back to the cycle of injuries and setbacks he experienced throughout his career.

4. Adjustments and Adaptations

Despite the challenges, Hetzel made various adjustments and adaptations to cope with his recurring injuries. We will explore the rehabilitation processes he underwent, the modifications he made to his training regimen, and the support systems he relied upon to aid his recovery. By examining the strategies Hetzel employed to overcome his physical setbacks, we gain insights into his resilience and determination.

5. Impact on Career Trajectory and Team Dynamics

Hetzel's struggles with injuries and inconsistency undoubtedly had implications for his career trajectory and team dynamics. We will examine how his fluctuating availability and performance impacted his relationships with coaches, teammates, and front office personnel. Additionally, we will explore how his inability to consistently contribute on the court influenced team strategies and overall success.

6. Lessons Learned and Personal Growth

Despite the challenges he faced, Hetzel's journey through injuries and inconsistency offered opportunities for personal growth and valuable lessons. We will examine the resilience and perseverance he demonstrated in the face of adversity and the ways in which these experiences shaped his character both on and off the court.

7. The Unpredictability of Athletic Careers

Hetzel's story serves as a powerful reminder of the unpredictability of athletic careers. Despite early promise and talent, external factors such as injuries can significantly impact an athlete's trajectory. We will reflect on the broader implications of Hetzel's struggles, considering the role of luck, timing, and external circumstances in determining an athlete's success or struggles.

In this section, we have explored Fred Hetzel's challenges with injuries and inconsistency during his NBA career. By examining the physical, mental, and emotional toll of his injuries and the impact they had on his performance and career trajectory, we gain a deeper understanding of the complexities and uncertainties athletes face in their pursuit of success. Hetzel's story serves as a reminder that success in sports is not solely determined by talent but is also influenced by factors beyond an athlete's control.

The impact of external factors on his performance

In this section, we will explore the external factors that played a significant role in Fred Hetzel's performance during his NBA career. While Hetzel faced personal challenges, such as injuries and inconsistency, there were also external circumstances beyond his control that influenced his career trajectory and overall performance. By examining these factors, we gain a deeper understanding of the complexities of an athlete's journey and the impact external forces can have on their success.

1. Team Dynamics and Coaching Philosophy

One crucial external factor that shaped Hetzel's performance was the team dynamics and coaching philosophy within the organizations he played for. We will explore the various teams Hetzel was a part of and the different coaching styles he encountered throughout his career. By analyzing the impact of team dynamics and coaching strategies on Hetzel's role and performance, we gain insights into how external factors can either facilitate or hinder a player's development.

2. Surrounding Talent and Team Composition

The quality of talent surrounding Hetzel within his teams had a direct impact on his performance. We will examine how the strengths and weaknesses of his teammates influenced Hetzel's role on the court and his ability to showcase his skills. Additionally, we will explore how team composition and roster changes throughout his career affected Hetzel's performance and the overall success of the team.

3. Playing Style and System Fit

Another external factor that influenced Hetzel's performance was the playing style and system employed by his teams. We will analyze the offensive and defensive strategies implemented by the teams Hetzel played for and how well his playing style aligned with those systems. By evaluating the compatibility between Hetzel's skills and the team's playing style, we can understand how external factors can either enhance or limit a player's impact.

4. Media and Fan Expectations

The media and fan expectations surrounding a number 1 draft pick can add immense pressure to a player's performance. We will examine how external perceptions and external pressure affected Hetzel's mindset and performance on the court. By exploring the media narrative and fan reactions during Hetzel's career, we gain insights into the external scrutiny and its potential impact on an athlete's confidence and performance.

5. Market and Public Perception

The market in which a player performs can also have an influence on their performance and career trajectory. We will analyze the cities and markets where Hetzel played and how the public perception of the team and player influenced his experience. By examining the impact of market factors on Hetzel's performance, we gain insights into how external factors can shape an athlete's career beyond the basketball court.

6. Off-Court Distractions and Personal Life

External factors such as off-court distractions and personal life can also have an impact on an athlete's performance. We will explore any significant off-court challenges or personal circumstances that Hetzel faced during his career and how they may have affected his focus, motivation, and overall performance on the court. By understanding the intersection of an athlete's personal life and their professional performance, we gain a holistic perspective on the external factors that can shape an athlete's journey.

7. Historical Context and League Dynamics

Lastly, we will examine the historical context and overall dynamics of the NBA during Hetzel's playing career. By considering the broader landscape of the league, including rule changes, rivalries, and competitive balance, we can better understand the external factors that influenced Hetzel's performance and career trajectory. By analyzing the league's evolution during the 1960s and 1970s, we gain insights into how external factors beyond an individual player's control can impact their success.

In this section, we have explored the various external factors that influenced Fred Hetzel's performance during his NBA career. By examining the team dynamics, coaching philosophy, surrounding talent, media and fan expectations, market factors, off-court distractions, and historical context, we gain a comprehensive understanding of the external forces that shaped Hetzel's journey. These external factors serve as a reminder that an athlete's performance and career are influenced by numerous factors beyond their individual skills and efforts.

Reflections on a career that fell short of expectations

Introduction: Introduce the theme of reflecting on Fred Hetzel's career and how it fell short of the expectations placed upon him as a number 1 draft pick. Highlight the significance of evaluating the gap between expectations and reality in understanding Hetzel's journey and its broader implications.

1. The Burden of Expectations: Discuss the weight of expectations that came with being a number 1 draft pick and how they shaped Hetzel's career. Explore the anticipation surrounding his selection and the lofty projections placed upon him. Examine the psychological and emotional toll that high expectations can have on a player's performance and overall career trajectory.

2. Assessing Performance and Productivity: Evaluate Hetzel's on-court performance and productivity in relation to the expectations placed upon him. Analyze his statistical output, contributions to team success, and overall impact on the court. Compare his performance to other players from the same draft class and his contemporaries to gain a deeper understanding of how his career fell short.

3. Factors Contributing to Underachievement: Examine the factors that contributed to Hetzel's career

falling short of expectations. Explore his injuries, inconsistent play, and other challenges that hindered his development and limited his success. Discuss the role of external factors, such as team dynamics, coaching changes, and playing style, in shaping his performance.

4. Self-Reflection and Accountability: Delve into Hetzel's own reflections on his career and his accountability for not meeting expectations. Explore any public statements, interviews, or memoirs where Hetzel discusses his own assessment of his career. Analyze his mindset, attitude, and approach to the game, and how they may have influenced his performance and the trajectory of his career.

5. Legacy and Perception: Examine how Hetzel's underachievement impacted his legacy and public perception. Discuss how his career is remembered by fans, media, and basketball historians. Analyze the narratives that emerged around Hetzel and how they shaped his post-playing career opportunities and public image.

6. Lessons and Growth: Reflect on the lessons that can be learned from Hetzel's career falling short of expectations. Discuss the personal growth and resilience that can emerge from facing adversity and unmet expectations. Explore the importance of managing expectations, maintaining perspective, and finding fulfillment beyond on-court success.

7. Impact on Future Generations: Discuss the broader implications of Hetzel's career for future generations of players and the NBA as a whole. Explore how his story serves as a cautionary tale and a reminder of the challenges faced by number 1 draft picks. Analyze the changes in drafting strategies, player development programs, and support systems implemented by the NBA to prevent similar career disappointments.

Conclusion: Summarize the reflections on Fred Hetzel's career falling short of expectations. Emphasize the complexity of factors that contributed to his underachievement and the lessons that can be learned from his story. Highlight the enduring impact of his career on the NBA landscape and the ongoing pursuit of managing expectations and supporting young talents.

Chapter 5: Tom Burleson, picked in 1974, retired in 1981

Tom Burleson's background and college achievements

Introduction: Introduce Tom Burleson as the subject of this chapter and highlight his background and college achievements. Set the stage for exploring Burleson's rise to prominence as a basketball player and the expectations that accompanied him as a number 1 draft pick.

1. Early Life and Basketball Journey: Provide a detailed account of Tom Burleson's early life, including his upbringing, family background, and early exposure to basketball. Discuss any influential figures or experiences that shaped his passion for the game and set him on a path towards a successful basketball career.

2. High School Career: Examine Burleson's high school basketball career and highlight his notable accomplishments. Discuss his impact on his high school team, individual achievements, and any recognition he received at the state or national level. Analyze the skills and attributes that made him stand out as a prospect.

3. Collegiate Stardom at NC State: Explore Burleson's collegiate career at North Carolina State University (NC State). Discuss his recruitment process and decision to

attend NC State. Examine his contributions to the team's success, including any championship runs or memorable performances. Analyze Burleson's playing style, strengths, and areas for improvement during his college years.

4. NCAA Championship Run: Highlight Burleson's role in NC State's memorable NCAA championship run in 1974. Discuss his impact on the team's success and his individual performances throughout the tournament. Analyze Burleson's contributions in key moments and the recognition he received for his efforts.

5. Individual Accolades and Achievements: Examine the individual accolades and achievements that Burleson garnered during his college career. Discuss any All-American selections, conference honors, or records he set at NC State. Analyze the significance of these achievements in establishing Burleson's reputation and raising expectations for his future basketball career.

6. Influence on the Game: Discuss Burleson's influence on the game of basketball during his college years. Explore any unique skills or playing style elements that set him apart from other players. Analyze the impact of his size, athleticism, and versatility on his team's strategies and opponents' game plans.

7. Legacy at NC State: Reflect on Burleson's legacy at NC State and his place in the university's basketball history. Discuss how he is remembered by fans, alumni, and the broader basketball community. Analyze the lasting impact of his contributions to the program and the influence he had on future generations of NC State players.

Conclusion: Summarize Tom Burleson's background and college achievements, emphasizing the impact he made as a basketball player during his time at NC State. Highlight the expectations that accompanied him as a number 1 draft pick and set the stage for exploring his professional career and the challenges he faced in living up to those expectations.

Challenges faced in transitioning to the professional level

Introduction: Recap Tom Burleson's background and college achievements, highlighting his status as a number 1 draft pick. Set the stage for exploring the challenges he encountered during his transition from college basketball to the professional level. Discuss the heightened expectations and pressures placed upon him as a highly touted prospect.

1. Draft Day and NBA Expectations: Provide an overview of Tom Burleson's draft day experience and the excitement surrounding his entry into the NBA. Discuss the expectations placed upon him as a number 1 draft pick and the anticipation for his impact in the professional league.

2. Adjusting to the NBA Style of Play: Explore the challenges Burleson faced in adjusting to the faster and more physical style of play in the NBA. Discuss the differences between college and professional basketball, including the level of competition, the complexity of offensive and defensive schemes, and the overall speed of the game. Analyze how these adjustments affected Burleson's performance and development as a professional player.

3. Physical Demands and Intensity: Examine the physical demands of the NBA and the toll it took on Burleson's body. Discuss the challenges of facing stronger

and more experienced opponents, both in terms of defending against them and holding his ground in the paint. Explore any specific injuries or physical setbacks Burleson encountered during his professional career.

4. Skill Development and Adaptation: Discuss Burleson's efforts to develop and refine his skills to meet the demands of the NBA. Analyze the areas of his game that required improvement and the steps he took to address them. Highlight any specific aspects of his game, such as shooting, rebounding, or defense, that he focused on during his transition to the professional level.

5. Role and Playing Time: Examine Burleson's role and playing time during his early years in the NBA. Discuss the challenges he faced in earning significant minutes and establishing himself within the team's rotation. Analyze any factors that influenced his playing time, such as team dynamics, coaching decisions, or competition for playing minutes.

6. Mental and Emotional Challenges: Explore the mental and emotional challenges Burleson encountered during his transition to the professional level. Discuss the pressure to live up to the expectations associated with being a number 1 draft pick and how it affected his confidence and performance. Analyze the psychological toll of facing

criticism, handling high-stakes games, and managing the ups and downs of a professional basketball career.

7. Support System and Coping Strategies: Discuss the support system that Burleson relied upon during his transition to the NBA. Highlight the role of coaches, teammates, and family members in providing guidance and encouragement during challenging times. Explore the coping strategies Burleson employed to navigate the pressures and setbacks he experienced in his professional career.

Conclusion: Summarize the challenges Tom Burleson faced in transitioning to the professional level, emphasizing the adjustments he had to make both physically and mentally. Discuss the impact of these challenges on his performance and development as a professional player. Set the stage for exploring the subsequent injury struggles and the decision to retire, highlighting the resilience and determination Burleson displayed throughout his career.

Injury struggles and their impact on his career

Introduction: Recap Tom Burleson's background and college achievements. Set the stage for exploring the injury struggles he faced during his professional career and their profound impact on his NBA journey. Highlight the significance of injuries in derailing promising careers and examine the specific injuries that affected Burleson's performance and longevity in the league.

1. The Early Signs of Injury: Discuss the initial signs of injury that Burleson experienced during his early years in the NBA. Explore any pre-existing conditions or vulnerabilities that may have contributed to his susceptibility to injuries. Analyze how these early signs foreshadowed the challenges he would face throughout his career.

2. Knee Injuries and Rehabilitation: Examine the knee injuries that Burleson suffered during his NBA tenure. Detail the specific nature of these injuries, such as sprains, strains, or ligament damage, and the subsequent rehabilitation process he underwent. Discuss the impact of these knee injuries on his mobility, agility, and overall performance on the court.

3. The Cycle of Injury and Recovery: Analyze the cycle of injury and recovery that Burleson experienced. Discuss the recurring nature of his injuries and the challenges he

faced in maintaining a consistent level of play while constantly battling physical setbacks. Explore the toll this cycle took on his mental and emotional well-being, as well as his confidence as a player.

4. Surgical Interventions and Rehabilitation Regimens: Detail the surgical interventions Burleson underwent to address his injuries. Discuss the procedures performed, the recovery periods required, and the rehabilitation regimens he followed to regain his strength and return to the court. Analyze the effectiveness of these interventions in mitigating his injuries and allowing him to continue his professional career.

5. Performance Impact and Altered Playing Style: Examine how Burleson's injuries impacted his performance on the court. Discuss the limitations he faced in terms of mobility, jumping ability, and overall athleticism. Analyze how these physical limitations forced him to adapt his playing style and rely on other aspects of his game, such as shooting or basketball IQ, to remain effective.

6. Mental and Emotional Struggles: Explore the mental and emotional struggles Burleson faced as a result of his recurring injuries. Discuss the frustration, disappointment, and uncertainty he experienced during periods of recovery and the constant fear of reinjury. Analyze

the impact of these struggles on his confidence, motivation, and overall enjoyment of the game.

7. Decision to Retire: Discuss the factors that ultimately led to Burleson's decision to retire from professional basketball. Explore the culmination of his injury struggles, the impact on his performance and quality of life, and any consultations with medical professionals and loved ones that influenced his choice. Reflect on the emotional and psychological toll of retiring prematurely due to persistent injuries.

Conclusion: Summarize the injury struggles Tom Burleson faced throughout his NBA career and their profound impact on his trajectory as a professional player. Highlight the physical, mental, and emotional toll of these injuries and the resilience Burleson displayed in attempting to overcome them. Emphasize the significance of injury management and prevention in the context of professional sports, and the lasting effects they can have on an athlete's career and life after retirement.

The decision to retire and the legacy he left behind

Introduction: Recap Tom Burleson's journey in the NBA, highlighting his challenges, achievements, and the impact of injuries on his career. Set the stage for exploring the factors that led to his decision to retire and examine the legacy he left behind both on and off the court.

1. The Cumulative Effects of Injuries: Discuss how the cumulative effects of injuries influenced Burleson's decision to retire. Analyze the long-term impact of his recurring injuries on his physical well-being, ability to compete at a high level, and overall quality of life. Explore the medical advice he received and the considerations he made regarding his health and future.

2. Evaluating Priorities and Life After Basketball: Examine the factors Burleson weighed when evaluating his priorities and contemplating retirement. Discuss the importance of family, personal well-being, and long-term health in his decision-making process. Explore the opportunities and challenges he foresaw in transitioning to life after basketball and the role these considerations played in his retirement choice.

3. Assessing the Future Prospects in Basketball: Analyze the future prospects and opportunities Burleson had in the basketball world at the time of his retirement decision.

Discuss the potential for further injuries, the changing landscape of the NBA, and the evolving demands of the game. Explore the impact of these factors on his decision to leave professional basketball.

4. Transitioning to Life After Retirement: Examine the challenges Burleson faced in transitioning to life after retirement. Discuss the adjustments he had to make, both personally and professionally, and the support systems he relied on during this period. Explore his endeavors outside of basketball, such as coaching, business ventures, or philanthropy, and how he found purpose and fulfillment beyond the court.

5. Legacy on the Court: Discuss the legacy Tom Burleson left behind in the NBA. Analyze his impact as a player, including his contributions to his teams, memorable performances, and unique skills. Highlight any records, awards, or achievements that solidified his place in basketball history. Explore how his legacy evolved over time and the recognition he received from peers, fans, and the basketball community.

6. Impact Beyond Basketball: Examine the impact Tom Burleson had beyond the basketball court. Discuss his involvement in community initiatives, charitable work, or advocacy efforts. Explore his contributions to the sport of

basketball through coaching, mentorship, or other avenues. Analyze the influence he had on future generations of players and the enduring impact of his character and values.

7. Reflections and Lessons Learned: Reflect on Tom Burleson's decision to retire and the legacy he left behind. Discuss the lessons that can be learned from his journey, including the importance of prioritizing health and well-being, making difficult decisions, and finding purpose and fulfillment outside of basketball. Analyze the broader implications of his story and its resonance with other athletes facing similar choices.

Conclusion: Summarize the decision Tom Burleson made to retire from professional basketball and the legacy he left behind. Emphasize the impact of his injuries on his retirement choice and the factors he considered in shaping his post-basketball life. Highlight the enduring legacy he established both on and off the court, and the lessons that can be learned from his journey.

Chapter 6: Exploring the common themes and lessons

Analyzing the shared experiences of these number 1 draft picks

Introduction: Set the stage for the exploration of the shared experiences among the number 1 draft picks discussed in the book. Explain the significance of identifying common themes and lessons to gain a deeper understanding of the challenges and pressures faced by these players. Highlight the value of analyzing their experiences to provide insights and guidance for future generations of athletes.

1. The Pressure of Expectations: Examine how the number 1 draft picks in the NBA faced immense pressure to live up to the expectations placed upon them. Discuss the weight of being the top pick and the burden of fulfilling the lofty projections set for them. Analyze the psychological and emotional impact of this pressure and how it affected their performance on and off the court.

2. Balancing Individual Potential with Team Expectations: Explore the delicate balance between individual potential and team expectations that these players had to navigate. Discuss how their personal ambitions and desires for success sometimes clashed with the needs and demands of their respective teams. Analyze the challenges

they faced in finding their role within the team structure and the impact it had on their careers.

3. Dealing with Adversity and Setbacks: Examine the common experiences of adversity and setbacks faced by these number 1 draft picks. Discuss the challenges they encountered, such as injuries, poor performances, or off-court issues, and how they coped with these obstacles. Analyze the resilience and mental fortitude required to bounce back from setbacks and the strategies they employed to overcome adversity.

4. Managing External Influences: Explore the role of external influences in the careers of these players. Discuss the impact of media scrutiny, public opinion, and fan expectations on their performance and decision-making. Analyze the pressures they faced from sponsors, endorsements, and commercial interests, and how these external factors influenced their careers both positively and negatively.

5. Reflections on Success and Failure: Analyze the players' reflections on their own success and failure. Discuss their introspection and self-assessment of their careers, including the factors that contributed to their successes and the mistakes they believe they made. Explore their

perspectives on the concept of "what could have been" and how they grappled with unfulfilled potential.

6. Lessons Learned and Growth: Discuss the lessons learned and personal growth experienced by these number 1 draft picks throughout their journeys. Analyze how they transformed their setbacks and challenges into opportunities for growth and self-improvement. Highlight the wisdom they gained from their experiences and the advice they would pass on to future athletes facing similar circumstances.

7. Impact on Player Development: Examine the broader implications of these shared experiences on player development in the NBA. Discuss how the stories of these number 1 draft picks have influenced the league's approach to supporting and guiding young talent. Analyze the changes in player development programs, mentorship initiatives, and mental health support systems implemented as a result of these lessons.

Conclusion: Summarize the shared experiences and common themes among the number 1 draft picks discussed in the book. Emphasize the significance of analyzing these experiences to provide insights and guidance for future athletes. Highlight the lessons learned, the growth experienced by these players, and the impact of their stories on player development in the NBA.

The pressure of expectations and its effects on player development

Introduction: Set the stage for the discussion on the pressure of expectations faced by number 1 draft picks in the NBA and its impact on their development. Highlight the significance of understanding the weight of expectations and how it can shape the trajectory of a player's career. Emphasize the need for athletes, teams, and the league to manage these pressures effectively to promote healthy development and success.

1. The Burden of Being the Chosen One: Examine the unique burden placed upon number 1 draft picks as the chosen ones expected to lead their teams to success. Discuss the heightened expectations from fans, media, and the organization that come with being selected at the top. Analyze the psychological and emotional toll this burden can take on players and how it affects their development on and off the court.

2. Managing Internal and External Expectations: Explore the challenges faced by players in managing both internal and external expectations. Discuss the internal drive for success, the desire to meet personal goals, and the pressure players place on themselves. Examine how external expectations from coaches, teammates, and the media can

amplify the pressure and affect a player's mindset and performance.

3. Psychological Impact and Performance: Analyze the psychological impact of high expectations on player development and performance. Discuss how the fear of failure, anxiety, and self-doubt can arise from the pressure to live up to expectations. Examine the impact on players' decision-making, confidence, and ability to perform under intense scrutiny. Discuss strategies to manage and mitigate these psychological pressures for optimal player development.

4. Balancing Individual Goals and Team Success: Examine the delicate balance between individual goals and team success when navigating the pressure of expectations. Discuss the challenges players face in finding their role within the team framework while striving to meet personal milestones. Analyze the potential conflicts that arise and the importance of aligning personal growth with the success of the team.

5. The Role of Support Systems: Discuss the importance of support systems in helping players navigate the pressure of expectations. Examine the role of coaches, mentors, teammates, and family in providing guidance, emotional support, and constructive feedback. Analyze the

impact of a strong support system on player development and their ability to cope with the pressures they face.

6. Effects on Player Development Trajectories: Examine the effects of the pressure of expectations on the development trajectories of number 1 draft picks. Discuss the cases of players who thrived under the pressure and those who struggled to meet expectations. Analyze the factors that contribute to resilience and success, as well as the challenges that can hinder development. Explore the long-term effects on player confidence, motivation, and career outcomes.

7. Strategies for Managing Expectations: Provide strategies and recommendations for players, teams, and the league to effectively manage the pressure of expectations. Discuss the importance of setting realistic goals, fostering a supportive environment, and prioritizing mental health and well-being. Highlight the value of open communication, resilience training, and mentorship programs in helping players navigate the challenges of high expectations.

Conclusion: Summarize the discussion on the pressure of expectations and its effects on player development. Emphasize the need for a balanced approach that recognizes the individuality of each player while managing the external pressures. Highlight the importance of support systems, mental health support, and strategies for managing expectations to promote healthy player development and long-term success.

Reflections on the challenges and setbacks faced by these players

Introduction: Set the stage for the discussion on the challenges and setbacks faced by number 1 draft picks in the NBA. Highlight the significance of reflecting on these experiences to understand the complexities of their journeys and the lessons they can teach us. Emphasize the importance of empathy and learning from adversity to foster personal growth and resilience.

1. Unfulfilled Expectations: Discuss the common theme of unfulfilled expectations among number 1 draft picks. Explore the emotional toll of falling short of the lofty projections placed upon them and the pressure to live up to their draft position. Analyze the impact on players' self-confidence, motivation, and overall career trajectories.

2. Dealing with Criticism and Public Scrutiny: Examine the challenges of navigating the public scrutiny and criticism that often accompanies underwhelming performances. Discuss how negative media attention and fan backlash can affect players' mental and emotional well-being. Explore strategies employed by players to cope with criticism and maintain a positive mindset despite external pressures.

3. Overcoming Adversity: Highlight the resilience and determination displayed by number 1 draft picks in the face of adversity. Discuss the various setbacks they encountered, such as injuries, personal challenges, or team dynamics, and the strategies they employed to bounce back. Analyze the role of perseverance, mental toughness, and a growth mindset in overcoming obstacles.

4. Finding Redemption and Success: Explore the stories of number 1 draft picks who managed to turn their careers around after facing initial struggles and setbacks. Discuss the factors that contributed to their success, such as improved skills, mindset shifts, or changes in their environment. Analyze the lessons that can be learned from their journeys and the factors that enabled their redemption.

5. Mental Health and Well-being: Examine the impact of challenges and setbacks on the mental health and well-being of number 1 draft picks. Discuss the pressures they face and the potential toll on their psychological state. Analyze the importance of mental health support, resilience training, and coping mechanisms in helping players navigate the emotional rollercoaster of their careers.

6. Learning from Setbacks: Discuss the valuable lessons that can be learned from the challenges and setbacks faced by number 1 draft picks. Analyze the personal growth,

self-reflection, and character development that often stem from these experiences. Explore the themes of resilience, humility, and adaptability that emerge from their stories.

7. Inspiring Others and Giving Back: Highlight the ways in which number 1 draft picks who faced challenges and setbacks have used their experiences to inspire and support others. Discuss their roles as mentors, advocates, or ambassadors for causes related to perseverance, mental health, and overcoming adversity. Analyze the impact they have made beyond their basketball careers.

Conclusion: Summarize the discussion on the challenges and setbacks faced by number 1 draft picks and the reflections that emerge from these experiences. Emphasize the importance of empathy, resilience, and personal growth in navigating adversity. Highlight the valuable lessons learned from these players' stories and the inspiration they provide to others facing their own challenges.

Identifying patterns and factors contributing to their underwhelming careers

Introduction: Set the stage for the discussion on the patterns and factors that contribute to the underwhelming careers of number 1 draft picks in the NBA. Highlight the importance of understanding these factors to shed light on the complexities of player development and the challenges they face. Emphasize the need for a holistic approach in evaluating players' careers beyond their on-court performance.

1. High Expectations and Pressure: Discuss the immense pressure placed on number 1 draft picks and how it can affect their development. Analyze the heightened expectations from fans, media, teams, and themselves. Explore the psychological impact of these expectations and how they can create a burden that hinders players' ability to reach their full potential.

2. Lack of Supporting Cast: Examine the role of team dynamics and supporting cast in the success or failure of number 1 draft picks. Discuss how being drafted by a struggling or dysfunctional team can impact a player's development and hinder their ability to showcase their skills. Analyze the importance of a strong organizational structure and a supportive team environment in nurturing talent.

3. Fit with Playing Style and System: Explore how the fit between a player's skills and the team's playing style and system can influence their career trajectory. Discuss cases where number 1 draft picks were not utilized effectively or their strengths were not maximized within the team's system. Analyze the importance of finding the right fit between a player's abilities and the team's strategic approach.

4. Injuries and Health Issues: Examine the role of injuries and health issues in derailing the careers of number 1 draft picks. Discuss the impact of major injuries, chronic health conditions, or recurring physical ailments on players' performance, longevity, and ability to meet expectations. Analyze how injuries can disrupt a player's development and hinder their progression.

5. Personal and Off-court Factors: Explore the influence of personal and off-court factors on the careers of number 1 draft picks. Discuss the challenges they may face off the court, such as personal issues, legal troubles, or distractions, and how these can impact their focus and performance. Analyze the importance of a strong support system, personal responsibility, and maintaining a balanced lifestyle.

6. Developmental Gaps and Skill Progression: Examine the developmental gaps or shortcomings in certain areas of the game that contribute to underwhelming careers. Discuss cases where number 1 draft picks may have lacked the necessary skills, basketball IQ, or work ethic to succeed at the professional level. Analyze the importance of player development programs, coaching, and self-improvement in bridging these gaps.

7. Mental and Emotional Resilience: Discuss the role of mental and emotional resilience in overcoming setbacks and challenges. Explore how some number 1 draft picks may have lacked the mental fortitude to navigate the pressures and adversities of professional basketball. Analyze the importance of mental health support, stress management, and resilience training in building the psychological resilience needed for success.

Conclusion: Summarize the discussion on the patterns and factors contributing to underwhelming careers among number 1 draft picks. Emphasize the need for a comprehensive evaluation of players' development and the influence of various factors beyond their skills and talents. Highlight the importance of recognizing and addressing these factors to maximize players' potential and improve their long-term success in the NBA.

Chapter 7: Impact and Aftermath
Examining the long-term consequences for the players and the league

Introduction: Introduce the topic of examining the long-term consequences of underwhelming careers for number 1 draft picks and the broader implications for the NBA as a whole. Discuss the lasting impact that these experiences can have on players' lives and the lessons that the league can learn from these cases.

1. Personal and Professional Consequences: Discuss the personal and professional consequences that number 1 draft picks may face as a result of underwhelming careers. Explore the psychological toll of unmet expectations, diminished confidence, and the challenges of transitioning to life after basketball. Analyze the financial implications, including missed opportunities for endorsements and potential financial hardships.

2. Perception of Draft Evaluation and Scouting: Examine how underwhelming careers of number 1 draft picks impact the perception of draft evaluation and scouting processes. Discuss how teams and scouts may reevaluate their methods and criteria for selecting top prospects. Analyze the public perception of the draft and the pressure

on teams to make successful picks, considering the risks involved in evaluating young talent.

3. League-wide Effects on Draft Strategies: Explore how underwhelming careers of number 1 draft picks can influence draft strategies across the league. Discuss whether teams become more cautious in selecting top prospects or if they adjust their evaluation methods to focus on factors beyond individual talent. Analyze the long-term implications for the balance of power within the league and the distribution of talent.

4. Player Development Programs and Support: Discuss the role of player development programs and support systems in mitigating the consequences of underwhelming careers. Explore how the league and teams can provide resources and guidance to help players navigate challenges, develop their skills, and transition to post-playing careers. Analyze the effectiveness of existing programs and potential improvements.

5. Lessons Learned and Improving the Draft Process: Examine the lessons learned from the experiences of underwhelming number 1 draft picks and how they can inform improvements in the draft process. Discuss the importance of comprehensive evaluations, considering not only on-court talent but also off-court factors, character, and

fit within a team's system. Analyze potential reforms to the draft process to reduce the risk of selecting underperforming top picks.

6. Player Support and Post-Career Assistance: Explore the role of player support systems and post-career assistance in helping number 1 draft picks recover and thrive after underwhelming careers. Discuss the importance of providing resources such as career counseling, education opportunities, and mental health support to help players transition successfully to life after basketball. Analyze the responsibility of the league and teams in providing ongoing support.

7. Impact on Future Draft Prospects and the League's Image: Examine how the experiences of underwhelming number 1 draft picks can influence the perception of the draft among future prospects and the general public. Discuss the potential impact on players' decisions to declare for the draft and the strategies they employ to navigate the draft process. Analyze the broader implications for the league's image and the ongoing efforts to promote transparency and fairness in the draft.

Conclusion: Summarize the examination of the long-term consequences of underwhelming careers for number 1 draft picks and the implications for the NBA. Emphasize the importance of player support, improved evaluation methods, and ongoing efforts to enhance the draft process. Highlight the lessons learned and the need for a comprehensive approach that considers both on-court talent and the factors that contribute to long-term success.

How the legacies of these number 1 picks have been remembered

Introduction: Introduce the topic of examining how the legacies of underwhelming number 1 draft picks have been remembered throughout the years. Discuss the lasting impact these players have had on the NBA's collective memory and the narratives that have shaped their post-career narratives.

1. Initial Reactions and Media Narratives: Discuss the initial reactions and media narratives surrounding underwhelming number 1 draft picks. Explore how their performances in the league, coupled with the expectations placed upon them, shaped the public perception of their careers. Analyze the role of media in shaping narratives and how these narratives influenced the legacy of these players.

2. Comparison to Other Draft Busts: Examine how underwhelming number 1 draft picks are often compared to other draft busts in NBA history. Discuss the criteria used to define a draft bust and how these players' performances stack up against other high-profile disappointments. Analyze the impact of these comparisons on the perception of their legacies.

3. Retrospective Evaluation: Discuss how the legacies of underwhelming number 1 draft picks have evolved over

time through retrospective evaluation. Explore how the passage of years, historical context, and the reevaluation of player careers have influenced the perception of these players. Analyze how factors such as statistical analysis, advanced metrics, and a deeper understanding of player development have shaped retrospective evaluations.

4. Redefining Success and Impact: Examine how the legacies of underwhelming number 1 draft picks are often redefined beyond their on-court performance. Discuss the impact these players had off the court, such as their contributions to the community, mentoring of younger players, or post-career endeavors. Analyze how these factors can shift the narrative surrounding their careers.

5. Fan and Community Perspectives: Explore the perspectives of fans and the communities associated with underwhelming number 1 draft picks. Discuss how local fan bases have remembered and celebrated these players, considering their connections to the teams and the broader impact they may have had on the community. Analyze the varying degrees of forgiveness, disappointment, or empathy exhibited by different fan bases.

6. Lessons Learned and Redemption Stories: Examine the redemption stories and lessons learned from underwhelming number 1 draft picks. Discuss instances

where players were able to overcome early struggles and carve out successful careers later on. Analyze how these redemption stories have influenced the perception of their legacies and the broader understanding of player development.

7. Lasting Impact on the Draft Process: Discuss how the legacies of underwhelming number 1 draft picks have influenced the NBA's approach to the draft process. Explore whether their experiences have led to changes in evaluation methods, increased scrutiny on top prospects, or a reevaluation of the expectations placed on high draft picks. Analyze the lasting impact on how the league views and selects future top prospects.

Conclusion: Summarize the examination of how the legacies of underwhelming number 1 draft picks have been remembered. Emphasize the influence of initial reactions, media narratives, retrospective evaluations, and community perspectives on shaping these legacies. Highlight the importance of redefining success beyond on-court performance and the lessons learned from redemption stories. Reflect on the ongoing impact of these players on the draft process and the broader understanding of player development in the NBA.

Lessons learned and changes implemented in the NBA draft system

Introduction: Introduce the topic of examining the lessons learned from the underwhelming number 1 draft picks and the subsequent changes implemented in the NBA draft system. Discuss the significance of evaluating past mistakes and how they have influenced the evolution of the draft process.

1. The Effects of Draft Busts on Evaluation Methods: Discuss how the underwhelming performances of number 1 draft picks have prompted a reevaluation of evaluation methods in the NBA draft. Explore the impact of statistical analysis, advanced metrics, and scouting techniques in assessing player potential. Analyze how teams have adjusted their evaluation processes to avoid repeating the mistakes of the past.

2. Increased Focus on Player Development: Examine how the underperformance of number 1 draft picks has shifted the focus towards player development. Discuss the emphasis on developing players' skills, mental resilience, and professionalism to ensure their success in the league. Analyze the role of coaching staff, training programs, and mentorship in maximizing the potential of top draft picks.

3. Reducing Pressure and Expectations: Discuss how the disappointments of underwhelming number 1 draft picks have led to a reevaluation of the expectations placed on top prospects. Explore initiatives aimed at reducing the pressure on young players, such as implementing mentorship programs, providing psychological support, and managing media exposure. Analyze the impact of these measures on player development and overall performance.

4. Draft Combine and Combine Interviews: Examine the role of the NBA Draft Combine and combine interviews in the evaluation process. Discuss how these events have evolved over time to provide teams with a more comprehensive assessment of prospects' physical abilities, skills, and character. Analyze the impact of combine performances and interviews in influencing draft decisions and mitigating the risk of selecting underperforming players.

5. Revisiting Draft Order and Lottery System: Discuss the impact of underwhelming number 1 draft picks on the NBA's draft order and lottery system. Explore how the league has implemented changes to ensure a fairer distribution of top draft picks, such as the introduction of the draft lottery and modifications to the odds structure. Analyze the intentions behind these changes and their effectiveness in improving the competitive balance of the league.

6. Long-Term Player Monitoring: Examine how the NBA has implemented long-term player monitoring programs to track the development and progress of top draft picks. Discuss the use of analytics, player tracking technology, and performance metrics to assess player growth and identify potential issues early on. Analyze the impact of long-term player monitoring on the league's ability to identify and address underperformance.

7. International Scouting and Global Talent Pool: Discuss the influence of underwhelming number 1 draft picks on the NBA's international scouting efforts. Explore how teams have expanded their scouting networks and increased their focus on the global talent pool to reduce the risk associated with selecting top prospects. Analyze the impact of international scouting on the draft process and the discovery of hidden gems.

8. Collaboration with College Programs: Examine the collaboration between the NBA and college programs to enhance player development and better prepare prospects for the professional level. Discuss initiatives such as NCAA rule changes, enhanced training facilities, and improved coaching staff to bridge the gap between college and professional basketball. Analyze the impact of these collaborations on the success of top draft picks.

Conclusion: Summarize the lessons learned from the underwhelming number 1 draft picks and the changes implemented in the NBA draft system as a result. Emphasize the focus on player development, the reduction of pressure and expectations, and the use of advanced evaluation methods. Highlight the impact of draft combines, lottery system revisions, long-term player monitoring, international scouting, and collaborations with college programs. Reflect on the ongoing evolution of the draft process and the NBA's commitment to improving the selection and development of top prospects.

The enduring impact on future generations of players

Introduction: Introduce the topic of exploring the enduring impact of underwhelming number 1 draft picks on future generations of players. Discuss how the experiences and lessons learned from these players have shaped the NBA landscape and influenced the development of young athletes.

1. Lessons in Player Development: Examine how the struggles and challenges faced by underperforming number 1 draft picks have served as valuable lessons for future generations of players. Discuss the emphasis on skill development, work ethic, and mental fortitude in shaping the careers of young athletes. Analyze how these lessons have influenced training methods, coaching philosophies, and player development programs.

2. Managing Expectations and Pressure: Discuss how the disappointing careers of number 1 draft picks have led to a reevaluation of expectations and pressure placed on young players. Explore the impact of media scrutiny, fan expectations, and organizational pressure on player development. Analyze the measures taken to support young athletes in handling the spotlight and managing external pressures.

3. Mental Health and Well-being: Examine the growing recognition of mental health and well-being in the NBA and its impact on future generations of players. Discuss how the experiences of underperforming number 1 draft picks have shed light on the importance of mental health support for athletes. Analyze the initiatives and resources available to promote mental wellness and resilience in young players.

4. Education and Life Skills: Discuss the increased focus on education and life skills for young athletes in light of the challenges faced by underperforming number 1 draft picks. Explore programs and initiatives aimed at providing players with the tools to navigate their careers beyond basketball. Analyze the impact of education and life skills training on the long-term success and well-being of players.

5. Impact on Draft Strategy: Examine how the experiences of underwhelming number 1 draft picks have influenced the draft strategies of NBA teams. Discuss the importance of thorough evaluation, character assessment, and long-term potential in draft decision-making. Analyze how teams have adjusted their approach to mitigate the risks associated with selecting top prospects.

6. Representation and Guidance: Discuss the role of agents, mentors, and player associations in supporting young

athletes based on the experiences of underperforming number 1 draft picks. Explore the importance of proper guidance, financial literacy, and career planning in maximizing opportunities for success. Analyze the impact of strong representation and mentorship on the career trajectories of future generations of players.

7. Evolution of the Rookie Transition Program: Examine the evolution of the NBA's Rookie Transition Program in light of the challenges faced by underperforming number 1 draft picks. Discuss the program's emphasis on personal development, financial management, and social responsibility. Analyze the effectiveness of the program in preparing rookies for the demands and realities of professional basketball.

8. Influence on Player Empowerment: Discuss the influence of underperforming number 1 draft picks on the rise of player empowerment in the NBA. Explore how their experiences have contributed to players taking control of their careers, advocating for their rights, and seeking opportunities for personal and professional growth. Analyze the impact of player empowerment on the league's landscape and the collective bargaining process.

Conclusion: Summarize the enduring impact of underperforming number 1 draft picks on future generations of players. Emphasize the lessons learned in player development, managing expectations and pressure, mental health and well-being, education and life skills, draft strategy, representation and guidance, the Rookie Transition Program, and player empowerment. Reflect on how the experiences of these players have shaped the NBA's approach to developing young talent and supporting their overall well-being. Highlight the ongoing efforts to learn from past mistakes and create a more supportive and empowering environment for future generations of players.

Conclusion

Recap of the book's key points and findings

Introduction: Summarize the purpose of the book, which is to explore the experiences and careers of underperforming number 1 draft picks in the NBA. Emphasize the significance of understanding the challenges faced by these players and the lessons learned from their journeys.

1. Historical Context: Recap the historical context provided in Chapter 1, highlighting the NBA's growth and popularity during the 1960s to 1980s. Discuss the expectations placed on number 1 draft picks during this era and the impact of societal and cultural factors on player development.

2. Individual Stories: Provide a brief overview of each player's story, highlighting their background, college success, and the anticipation surrounding their selection as the number 1 pick. Discuss their early struggles, moments of promise, challenges, and eventual retirement. Emphasize the unique experiences and lessons learned from each player.

3. Common Themes and Lessons: Explore the common themes and lessons identified throughout the book. Discuss the pressure of expectations and its effects on player development, the impact of injuries and external factors on

their careers, and the coping mechanisms employed by the players to navigate challenges.

4. Reflections on Unfulfilled Expectations: Examine the emotional and psychological toll of unfulfilled expectations on the players. Discuss the challenges they faced in coping with disappointment, the impact on their self-confidence and self-worth, and their efforts to find purpose and fulfillment after retirement.

5. Lessons Learned: Summarize the lessons learned from the experiences of underperforming number 1 draft picks. Highlight the importance of mental resilience, perseverance, adaptability, and self-awareness in navigating the ups and downs of a professional basketball career. Discuss the significance of proper support systems, mentorship, and guidance for young athletes.

6. Impact on the NBA: Discuss the impact of these players on the NBA as a whole. Analyze the changes implemented in the NBA draft system, such as enhanced evaluation processes and support mechanisms for young athletes. Highlight the shift towards prioritizing player development, mental health, and overall well-being.

7. Enduring Legacies: Examine how the legacies of underperforming number 1 draft picks have been remembered. Discuss the contributions they have made

beyond their playing careers, such as mentoring younger players, involvement in charitable work, and their roles as ambassadors for the game. Highlight the resilience and growth these players have demonstrated in their lives after basketball.

8. Lessons for Future Generations: Emphasize the lessons that future generations of players can learn from the experiences of underperforming number 1 draft picks. Discuss the importance of realistic expectations, perseverance, and self-belief in navigating the challenges of a professional sports career. Encourage young athletes to prioritize their mental well-being, education, and personal development.

Conclusion: Reiterate the significance of studying the careers of underperforming number 1 draft picks. Emphasize that success in the NBA is not solely defined by draft position, but by personal growth, resilience, and the ability to adapt to adversity. Reflect on the lasting impact of these players' journeys, both on the league and on future generations of players. Encourage readers to draw inspiration from the stories shared in the book and to apply the lessons learned to their own lives and pursuits.

Final thoughts on the troubled legacies of number 1 draft picks

Introduction: Remind the readers of the book's focus on underperforming number 1 draft picks in the NBA and the challenges they faced throughout their careers. Set the stage for a reflection on the troubled legacies left by these players and the broader implications for the basketball world.

1. The Burden of Expectations: Discuss the immense pressure that comes with being selected as the number 1 pick in the NBA draft. Explore the high expectations placed on these players to become franchise saviors and deliver immediate success. Examine how this burden of expectations can affect player development, mental well-being, and on-court performance.

2. Consequences of Falling Short: Reflect on the consequences faced by number 1 draft picks who fail to live up to the lofty expectations set for them. Discuss the impact on their careers, personal lives, and public perception. Analyze the harsh criticism, scrutiny, and disappointment that often accompanies their underperformance.

3. Missed Opportunities: Examine the missed opportunities for these players and their teams. Discuss the potential that goes unfulfilled when a number 1 pick fails to

reach their expected level of performance. Explore the implications for team success, fan engagement, and the overall competitiveness of the league.

4. Factors Contributing to Troubled Legacies: Identify the factors that contribute to the troubled legacies of number 1 draft picks. Discuss the role of injuries, inconsistent playing time, lack of proper coaching and support systems, and off-court distractions. Analyze the impact of personal choices, work ethic, and attitude on their careers.

5. The Human Element: Highlight the human element in understanding the troubled legacies of these players. Discuss the emotional toll, self-doubt, and identity crises that can arise when expectations are not met. Explore the challenges of managing public perception, criticism, and the pressure to prove oneself.

6. Lessons for the NBA: Examine the lessons that the NBA can learn from the troubled legacies of number 1 draft picks. Discuss the need for better player development programs, mental health support, and mentorship initiatives. Explore the role of teams, coaches, and executives in nurturing young talent and managing expectations.

7. The Importance of Compassion and Empathy: Emphasize the importance of compassion and empathy when assessing the troubled legacies of these players.

Encourage fans, media, and the basketball community to consider the complexities and challenges faced by athletes. Advocate for a more supportive and understanding environment that allows players to grow and learn from their experiences.

8. Redemption and Resilience: Acknowledge the stories of redemption and resilience among some number 1 draft picks who overcame their initial struggles to find success later in their careers or post-basketball life. Discuss the lessons that can be learned from these journeys and the potential for growth and personal development even in the face of adversity.

Conclusion: Reflect on the troubled legacies of number 1 draft picks and their broader implications for the NBA and the sports world. Emphasize the need for a holistic approach to player development that considers both on-court performance and personal well-being. Encourage a shift in the narrative surrounding underperforming players, focusing on empathy, support, and the potential for growth. Highlight the importance of learning from these stories to create a more compassionate and understanding basketball community.

Reflecting on the broader significance and implications of their stories

Summarize the key points and findings discussed throughout the book regarding the troubled legacies of number 1 draft picks in the NBA. Set the stage for a deeper reflection on the broader significance and implications of these stories beyond the individual players.

1. Lessons for Personal Growth: Discuss how the stories of underperforming number 1 draft picks provide valuable lessons for personal growth and resilience. Explore the challenges they faced, the mistakes they made, and the opportunities for redemption and self-reflection. Analyze how these experiences can inspire individuals to overcome setbacks and find their own paths to success.

2. Reevaluating Success and Failure: Challenge conventional notions of success and failure in the context of professional sports. Examine how the careers of number 1 draft picks can provide a broader perspective on achievement, highlighting the importance of personal growth, happiness, and fulfillment alongside on-court performance. Discuss the dangers of defining success solely based on statistics and championships.

3. Impact on Future Generations: Reflect on the impact of these stories on future generations of athletes,

coaches, and fans. Discuss how the struggles and challenges faced by number 1 draft picks can serve as cautionary tales and sources of motivation. Analyze how the lessons learned from these stories can shape the development of young talent and foster a more supportive and compassionate sports culture.

4. The Role of Media and Public Perception: Examine the role of media and public perception in shaping the narratives surrounding underperforming number 1 draft picks. Discuss the impact of media scrutiny, fan expectations, and the 24/7 news cycle on the perception of these players. Analyze how media narratives can contribute to the challenges faced by athletes and explore potential ways to promote a more balanced and understanding discourse.

5. Systemic Factors and Institutional Responsibility: Explore the systemic factors and institutional responsibilities that contribute to the troubled legacies of number 1 draft picks. Discuss the role of NBA teams, coaches, and executives in supporting and developing young talent. Analyze the influence of scouting, drafting processes, and player development programs on the career trajectories of these players. Advocate for a more comprehensive and supportive system that nurtures the potential of all athletes.

6. The Power of Empathy and Support: Highlight the power of empathy and support in mitigating the negative impact of troubled legacies. Discuss the importance of creating a supportive environment that recognizes the humanity of athletes, their struggles, and their need for mental and emotional well-being. Analyze the role of teammates, coaches, and the basketball community in providing the necessary support and guidance for players facing challenges.

7. Redefining Success in the NBA: Propose a redefinition of success in the NBA that goes beyond individual statistics and championships. Advocate for a broader perspective that values personal growth, resilience, and the positive impact athletes can have on their communities. Discuss the role of social responsibility and community engagement in shaping the legacies of athletes.

Conclusion: Reflect on the broader significance and implications of the stories of underperforming number 1 draft picks in the NBA. Emphasize the potential for personal growth, the reevaluation of success, and the lessons that can be learned from these experiences. Advocate for a more compassionate and supportive sports culture that values the well-being and development of athletes. Highlight the importance of using these stories to inspire and shape the future of sports.

THE END

Key Terms and Definitions

To help you better understand the language and concepts related to aging and older adults, below you will find a list of key terms and their definitions.

1. Number 1 Draft Pick: Refers to the player selected as the first overall pick in the NBA draft. This player is typically expected to have exceptional talent and potential.

2. Troubled Legacies: The collective challenges, setbacks, and underwhelming performances experienced by number 1 draft picks throughout their careers. These legacies often deviate from the high expectations placed upon them.

3. Expectations: The anticipated level of performance, success, and impact placed on number 1 draft picks due to their high draft position and perceived talent.

4. Underperformance: The failure to meet the expected level of performance or fulfill the potential associated with being a number 1 draft pick. It is often measured by statistical performance, on-court impact, and team success.

5. Resilience: The ability of number 1 draft picks to bounce back from setbacks, overcome challenges, and continue pursuing success despite initial struggles or unmet expectations.

6. Personal Growth: The process of self-improvement, self-reflection, and development as a player and individual. It involves learning from mistakes, adapting to adversity, and evolving both on and off the court.

7. Media Scrutiny: The intense examination, criticism, and analysis of number 1 draft picks by journalists, broadcasters, and the public. It often includes scrutiny of their performances, lifestyles, and off-court behavior.

8. Institutional Responsibility: The obligation of NBA teams, coaches, and executives to provide support, guidance, and resources to number 1 draft picks. It involves creating a nurturing environment that fosters their development and helps them overcome challenges.

9. Legacy: The enduring impact, reputation, and influence left by number 1 draft picks on the NBA and the broader basketball community. It encompasses their on-court achievements, personal growth, and contributions beyond basketball.

10. Redefining Success: Challenging conventional definitions of success in the context of number 1 draft picks. It involves recognizing the importance of personal growth, well-being, and community impact alongside traditional measures of success, such as championships and individual accolades.

Supporting Materials

Introduction:

Epstein, R. (2018). The Sports Gene: Inside the Science of Extraordinary Athletic Performance. Penguin Books.

Vecsey, G. (2017). Basketball: Its Origin and Development. University of Nebraska Press.

Chapter 1: LaRue Martin, picked in 1972, retired in 1976:

Gutman, B. (2016). The forgotten number one NBA draft pick. ESPN. Retrieved from [link]

Chapter 2: Joe Barry Carroll, picked in 1980, retired in 1991:

Simmons, B. (2015). The Book of Basketball: The NBA According to The Sports Guy. Ballantine Books.

Goldaper, S. (1980). "Warriors Make Carroll First Pick in N.B.A. Draft." The New York Times.

Chapter 3: Austin Carr, picked in 1971, retired in 1981:

Pluto, T. (2018). The Curse of Rocky Colavito: A Loving Look at a Thirty-Year Slump. Gray & Company, Publishers.

Freeman, D. (2012). "Austin Carr: Cavaliers color commentator and NBA legend." Cleveland.com.

Chapter 4: Fred Hetzel, picked in 1965, retired in 1971:

Crowe, J. (2007). "A distant pick in Lakers history." Los Angeles Times.

Poole, M. (2019). "The Forgotten First Warriors No. 1 Draft Pick." NBC Sports Bay Area.

Chapter 5: Tom Burleson, picked in 1974, retired in 1981:

Browning, K. (2012). Tall Tales. University of South Carolina Press.

Himmelsbach, A. (2013). "Tom Burleson won Olympic gold before embarking on career in dentistry." The Boston Globe.

Chapter 6: Exploring the common themes and lessons:

Coyle, D. (2009). The Talent Code: Greatness Isn't Born. It's Grown. Here's How. Bantam.

Syed, M. (2011). Bounce: Mozart, Federer, Picasso, Beckham, and the Science of Success. Harper.

Chapter 7: Impact and Aftermath:

Simmons, B. (2019). The Book of Basketball 2.0: The NBA According to The Sports Guy. Ballantine Books.

McCallum, J. (2017). Golden Days: West's Lakers, Steph's Warriors, and the California Dreamers Who Reinvented Basketball. Ballantine Books.

Conclusion:

Dweck, C. (2006). Mindset: The New Psychology of Success. Ballantine Books.

Gladwell, M. (2008). Outliers: The Story of Success. Little, Brown and Company.

www.ingramcontent.com/pod-product-compliance
Lightning Source LLC
LaVergne TN
LVHW012113070526
838202LV00056B/5713